P9-DNI-106

A POCKET HISTORY OF
IRELAND

A POCKET HISTORY OF
IRELAND

JOSEPH McCULLOUGH

Gill & Macmillan

Contents

The Tomb Builders 6

The Celts 10

The Druids and the Fili 14

The Mythological Cycles 18

The Celtic Way of War 22

St. Patrick 26

The Monasteries 30

The Early Irish Saints 34

The Vikings 36

Brian Bórú and the Battle of Clontarf 42

The Norman Invasion 46

A Time of Mercenaries:
   Gallowglass and Kerns 50

Edward and Robert the Bruce 54

The Statutes of Kilkenny
   and the English Pale 58

The Kildares 62

The Irish Reformation
   and the Catholic Reaction 66

Desmond's Rebellions
   and the Munster Plantation 70

Tyrone's Rebellion 74

The Flight of the Earls
   and the Ulster Plantation 78

Black Tom Tyrant 82

The 1641 Rising and the
   Confederate Catholics of Ireland 86

Oliver Cromwell 90

The Cromwellian Land Settlement 94

The Williamite War and
   the Battle of the Boyne 98

The Treaty of Limerick
   and the Penal Laws 102

Jonathan Swift 106

The Rise of Irish Nationalism
   and Prosperity 110

Henry Grattan and the Volunteers 114

The Secret Societies: From the
   Whiteboys to the Orange Order 118

Wolfe Tone and the United Irishmen 122

General Lake and the Wexford War 126

The Act of Union 130

Robert Emmet 134

Daniel O'Connell,
   Liberator of the Nation 138

Young Ireland and the
   Repeal Movement 142

The Great Famine 146

The Irish Republican Brotherhood
   and the Fenians 150

William Gladstone 154

Charles Stewart Parnell 158

The Gaelic League and the
   Gaelic Athletic Association 162

William Butler Yeats 166

Constructive Unionism
   and the Home Rule Crisis 170

Ireland in the First World War 174

James Connolly 178

Patrick Henry Pearse, 182
   Poet and Revolutionary

The Easter Rising 186

Sinn Féin and the First Dáil 190

The Birth of the Irish Republican Army 194

The Black and Tans &
   the First Bloody Sunday 198

The Anglo-Irish Treaty 202

The Irish Civil War 206

The Death of Michael Collins 210

Partition 214

Fianna Fáil and the Irish Constitution 218

Ireland in the Second World War 222

The Withering of Ireland 226

The Celtic Tiger 230

The Civil Rights Movement
   and the Troubles 234

The Good Friday Agreement 238

An Island of Song, Dance and Poetry 242

Index 246

Further reading 254

Acknowledgments 256

The Tomb Builders

Although they left behind no stories or songs, Ireland's Stone Age settlers covered the island in hundreds of magnificent stone tombs.

HUNTER GATHERERS made tools out of stone and used them to hunt for food

In the year 8,000 BC, Ireland was an unpopulated wild green island, covered in forests and teeming with game. It was the Mesolithic Era, the Middle Stone Age, and most of Europe had already been settled. Then, on some unknown day between 8,000 and 7,000 BC, the first people stepped out of their primitive boats and on to Irish soil. These first people were hunters and gatherers, surviving mainly on what the land naturally provided. They fished and raised a few domesticated animals, including goats and sheep. They made rough pottery and tools out of stone. Around 4,000 BC a new people began to arrive, with new ideas. They would till the soil to raise cereal crops and build long wooden houses with their stone tools. They were Neolithic people, inhabitants of the New Stone Age, and slowly they displaced or absorbed the earlier Mesolithic people. Around this time the Irish erected the first of their great stone tombs.

The remains of over 1,000 megalithic tombs can still be found in Ireland, particularly in the north. These tombs, which offer clues as to the lives and culture of the Stone Age people of Ireland, are divided into four types: court tombs, passage tombs, portal tombs and wedge tombs. Each type roughly corresponds to a specific time or geography. Court tombs are the oldest known form of Irish stone construction. They usually consist of a rectangular cairn, constructed from dry stones.

Elsewhere, the settlers built passage tombs – long, rock-enclosed passages leading to a burial chamber.

Over 1,000 years after the first tombs, the Irish began building a third type: portal tombs.

NEOLITHIC TOOLS were fashioned from stone, chipped into a rough shape, then polished with an abrasive rock

The last variety of tomb built by the Stone Age Irish was the wedge tomb. Their beginning coincides with the arrival of a new group, the Beaker People, who often buried drinking beakers with their dead. The Beaker People were farmers and animal breeders who had unlocked the secrets of how to make metal tools.

With the arrival of the Bronze Age, new peoples, such as the Food Vessel folk, came to the island, and the old practice of tomb building faded away. However, these historically important structures help archaeologists to reconstruct the past, and serve as attractions for thousands of tourists every year.

NEWGRANGE TOMB
near Drogheda is one of the best examples of a passage tomb. Built in around 3,200 BC, it covers an area of over one acre

IRISH TOMBS

Court tombs

They were 25–35 metres long and contained an open courtyard surrounded by stone walls at one end, and one or two enclosed burial chambers at the other. Some were then covered with earth. Court tombs were built by the northern Irish, and they continued to construct them until the early years of the Bronze Age, around 2,000 BC.

Passage tombs

These are significant as they contain early examples of Irish artwork. Chiselled or carved into the walls of the tomb with sharpened rocks, this artwork is often composed of geometric patterns such as circles, swirls, triangles or zigzags. Today, the meaning of this artwork can only be guessed.

Portal tombs

These commonly consist of one chamber, often covered with a gigantic capstone, and a pair of large portal stones forming a doorway. How the Stone Age people constructed tombs with stones weighing upwards of 150 tons is still a heavily debated mystery.

Wedge tombs

These kinds of tombs first appeared around 2,200 BC, and their construction carried on well into the Bronze Age. The name derives from the roughly triangular shape of the tombs. Today, between 500 and 550 wedge tombs survive in Ireland, mainly in the north.

Detail of stone carvings at Newgrange entrance

The Celts

Along with their iron-based technology, the Celts brought a new culture to Ireland which, over the ensuing centuries, would evolve into the traditional Gaelic way of life.

CELTIC WARRIORS were the dominant power in Western Europe in the early Iron Age

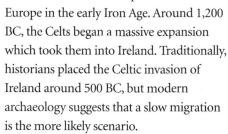

According to the Ancient Greeks, the people living in the Alpine regions to the north were *Keltoi*, meaning 'barbarians'; however, history now remembers these Celtic barbarians as the dominant power in Western Europe in the early Iron Age. Around 1,200 BC, the Celts began a massive expansion which took them into Ireland. Traditionally, historians placed the Celtic invasion of Ireland around 500 BC, but modern archaeology suggests that a slow migration is the more likely scenario.

The first Celts to arrive in Ireland are thought to have come from the Iberian Peninsula and settled in the south and the west. They spoke a language called Q-Celtic.

Over the following centuries these Celts mixed with the earlier inhabitants, slowly absorbing some of their language and culture. This linguistic evolution resulted in Irish Gaelic, the language that came to dominate the entire island. This language and its accompanying culture would eventually create a divide between the Irish Celts and those in the rest of Europe.

At some point, the Irish adopted the term Gaels in order to distinguish themselves from foreigners. This word may derive from the Welsh term for Irishman, *Gwyddel*, itself derived from the word for wild or savage. According to Irish legend, Gael comes from Gaedheal Glas, a grandson of the Biblical Noah, who created the Irish language.

CELTIC EXPANSION
began around 1,200 BC, sweeping through France and the Iberian Peninsula, across to Britain and eventually Ireland

Several hundred years after the Q-Celtic people arrived, another group of Celts came from Britain and settled in the North. Although culturally similar, these new people had made several advances, most notably in artwork. Unlike most European art, Celtic artwork made little attempt at realistic depiction. Instead it drew inspiration from the natural world to create intricate geometric patterns. This early art later developed into the maze-like tangles

GEOMETRIC DESIGNS were characterised by intricate designs and were commonly seen on Celtic crosses and jewellery

CELTIC SOCIETY

The Celts settled in small farming groups based around the family unit called the gelfhine. This consisted of all the male descendants of a common grandfather. Women became members of their husband's gelfhine. In times of crisis, a larger group, the derbfhine, would gather. Composed of the male descendants of a common great-grandfather, the derbfhine was the basic legal unit of Celtic society. Property belonged to the derbfhine rather than to one individual.

seen on Celtic crosses and jewellery. The Celts often displayed their artwork on jewellery such as torques, but it also adorned weaponry, where it may have served a heraldic or religious purpose. Eventually, the dominant Q-Celtic in the south absorbed these newcomers, adopting their cultural advancements, but supplanting their language.

According to archaeological record, the Celts arrived in Ireland gradually, and not as part of any invasion or mass migration. It is unlikely that the Celts ever outnumbered the Bronze Age Irish. But, perhaps because of the superiority of their iron-based techonology or because of the close organisation of their family units, their culture came to dominate the entire island, and brought all the inhabitants together into a Gaelic whole.

FAMILY GROUPS were based around a unit called the gelfhine and formed the basis of the numerous petty Celtic kingdoms

The Druids and the Fili

Although little is known about the druids or the fili, together they served Celtic society in the role of priests, prophets, judges and historians.

STONE CIRCLES
remain an archaeological mystery in Britain and Ireland

Within each clan or family unit in Celtic society, a definite hierarchy existed. From the king or chieftain down to the slaves, everyone knew his or her place. There was at least one group, however, that existed outside of this rigid structure, which acknowledged no king as master and which could move freely between the clans. They were the druids, and what little information exists about these mysterious figures raises more questions than it answers.

What can be said for certain is that the druids were the guardians of Celtic belief. Early Gaelic religion acknowledged a vast pantheon of gods, most of

THE ROMAN VIEW OF THE DRUIDS

In Britain and Gaul, the druids became the leaders of the resistance against the Roman invasions and came to be seen by the Romans as fanatic religious warriors. Although many druids probably fled to Ireland with the fall of the rest of the Celtic world, the Irish druids never developed any kind of militant reputation.

whom represented aspects of the natural world. The druids served as the keepers of this religious lore and as leaders of religious ceremonies. Additionally, many druids held positions as prophets or soothsayers, able to predict the future and thus give wise council. Finally, as a wise and learned class of people who stood outside the normal Celtic class structure, the druids served as judges and mediators.

When Christianity spread into Ireland, many druids challenged the new, upstart religion, but they did so intellectually, through debate. It is even probable that many druids adopted Christianity, or aspects of it, and worked it into their own belief system.

ROMAN SOLDIERS saw the druids as fanatic religious warriors

THE FILIDH

By the middle ages, the fili had merged with the bards to become both the keepers of knowledge and the great singers of praise-poetry. Chieftains often hired them to glorify their own deeds and the deeds of their ancestors. These later bards are normally termed filidh, and they too have left behind a large body of work.

DRUIDS SERVED as the keepers of religious lore

The fili were the poets of the Celts. It is not clear if these poets were an offshoot of the druids or a separate group altogether, but there were many similarities. Like the druids, the fili spent years studying and memorising ancient oral lore. But where the druids concentrated on spiritualism, the fili focused on the material world. They memorised histories, genealogies and the law. Although the fili composed and remembered this information as a form of poetry, they did not necessarily perform it. Their job was to preserve knowledge, not to entertain.

CHRISTIANITY
was responsible
for huge changes
in Gaelic society

With the coming of Christianity, Gaelic society underwent huge changes. Slowly the druids died out as a distinct class, overwhelmed by the church. Although it is possible that isolated druidic communities survived down to the middle ages, eventually they became extinct, and most of their orally preserved knowledge was lost. Some lore did survive, however, through the fili who persevered for many more centuries.

With the coming of the church, the fili took the Latin alphabet and used it to produce the first written works in the Irish language. It is thanks to the work of these fili that any of the ancient Irish history and mythology has survived to the present day.

Eventually, the systematic destruction of the Gaelic culture and language wiped out the fili just as it had done to the druids hundreds of years before. Although these two mysterious Gaelic orders have long since vanished, their spirit still lives on in many of the politicians, the lawyers, the artists, the craftsmen and the singers of modern Ireland.

The Mythological Cycles

Although the Celts left behind no true 'history', over 150 of their stories have survived and give us a glimpse into their ancient culture.

Ireland's greatest treasures are not made of gold or jewels. Instead they are manuscripts – old, damaged and incomplete. That these few books, dating from the middle ages, survive at all is nothing short of miraculous. Through fires, war, the dissolution of the monasteries and the suppression of the Irish language and culture, these ancient tomes endured, carrying with them the last of the Gaelic culture: the true stories of Ireland.

DEIRDRE OF THE Sorrows whose story is part of the Ulster Cycle

Today, there are just over 150 stories that have survived in various fragments and versions passed down from the days of the ancient Gaels. However, it wasn't until the early nineteenth century that German scholars

THE ULSTER CYCLE

The largest and best known of the mythological cycles is the Ulster Cycle, which contains 80 stories about the warriors and kings of the Ulaid – the people who gave their name to Ulster. The cycle is most famous for its stories of Ireland's greatest mythical hero, Cúchulainn. The son of a god and a mortal woman, Cúchulainn possesses super-human strength and is a warrior and a hurler without equal. It has been suggested that many of his stories served as a guide for young Irish warriors, giving lessons on honour and nobility. This theory is especially interesting because the story of Cúchulainn went on to inspire generations of Irish revolutionaries. In the Ulster Cycle, Cúchulainn is given a choice by a druid to live either a long life, or a short life that will always be remembered. Cúchulainn chooses the latter and, much like the leaders of the Easter Rising in 1916, his deeds became a part of Irish legend before sending him to his grave. The Ulster Cycle also contains the longest literary work in ancient Irish, the Táin Bó Cúailgne, which can, at best, be roughly translated as the 'Cattle Raid of Cooley'.

Cúchulainn and the
Cattle Raid of Cooley

THE FENIAN CYCLE

The second of the cycles, the Fenian Cycle, is a bit of a misnomer. The term 'Fenian' didn't come into being until the nineteenth century. These stories are grouped together because they all concern Fianna, groups of young warriors out seeking wealth and adventure. The main hero of these stories is Fionn Mac Cumhaill (Finn MacCool in English). Unlike stories in the other cycles, some of these survived down to the present in oral form, and were told not just in Ireland, but also in Scotland and the Isle of Man.

unlocked the code of ancient Irish grammar and were able once again to bring these stories fully to life. As part of their studies, they grouped the stories into cycles, based on the content and themes: the Ulster Cycle, the Fenian Cycle, the Mythological Cycle and the Cycle of Kings.

OISÍN AND NIAMH whose adventures are recounted in the Fenian Cycle

Today, the myths and legends of Ireland are safe. The manuscripts are protected in museums and libraries, and hundreds of copies and translations have been made. However, if not for the actions of a few unknown heroes, the greatest treasures of Ireland could easily have been lost forever.

THE MYTHOLOGICAL CYCLE

The Mythological Cycle is also a bit of a confusing name. While all of the ancient stories in question are usually considered Irish myths, these particular stories are deemed to have a stronger mythological bent than the others. In truth, compared to the mythologies of other cultures, the Irish myths contain very little fantasy. Perhaps this is because they were preserved by monks, or perhaps it is evidence that the Gaels saw a closer connection between their gods and their world. Either way, the stories in the Mythological Cycle relate the tales of the Irish gods and goddesses, but normally in the guise of powerful humans. They also tell of the various mythical invasions of Ireland by semi-human beings such as the Fir Bolg.

CHILDREN OF LIR is a well-known legend belonging to the Mythological Cycle

THE CYCLE OF KINGS

The last story grouping is the Cycle of Kings. It is a later, looser designation than the others, and includes stories about both mythical and historical kings, although separating fact from fiction in most cases is impossible.

The Celtic Way of War

Despite their beautiful poetry and artwork, the Celts were a warrior people who prized martial ability above all else.

While most historians now dismiss the idea of a massive Celtic invasion of Ireland, that does not mean their steady migration was peaceful. Using their superior bronze weapons, the Celts seized the best land in Ireland for themselves and pushed the previous inhabitants into the rougher corners of the island. In this environment, where wealth and power could be taken with the sword and spear, it is no surprise that Celtic culture placed warriors in the highest regard.

Most of what is known about the ancient Celtic warriors comes from three sources: archaeology, the ancient Irish myths and the Greeks and Romans who wrote about the Celts in Gaul (modern France) and Britain.

CELTIC WARRIOR
from the later period, when swords and armour were more common

NIALL OF THE NINE HOSTAGES

The greatest warrior king of the ancient Irish was Niall Noígiallach (Niall of the Nine Hostages). A semi-legendary figure, Niall dominated the Celtic tribes and led massive slave raids against Britain. He established his base at the Hill of Tara and from this seat founded the Uí Neill dynasty.

Through these sources, it is possible to paint a vivid picture of the lives and battles of the Celts.

At the local level, Celts would form warbands, consisting of the local chief, his kinsman and perhaps a few mercenary fighting men he could attract through gifts. These small warbands would often raid their neighbours, most often to steal cattle, but occasionally taking slaves. As certain chiefs grew stronger, they used intimidation or gifts to attract allied warbands and thus form armies. The more warbands a chief could summon to his cause, the more power he wielded. Some chieftains became powerful enough to be called kings and led armies against the other Celtic kingdoms,

STONE ARTEFACT
from the Celtic period

CELTIC WEAPONS

Most Celts fought with spears: short light spears for throwing, and longer, heavier spears for hand-to-hand. Swords were highly prized among the Celts, but their cost limited their use to only the wealthiest warriors. For protection they carried large wooden and bronze shields, and a few might have had helmets. Armour was uncommon among the Celts, but became more widely used in the later periods. Bows and slings were also employed, but the unmanly nature of striking an enemy from a distance limited their appeal.

ROMAN LEGIONARIES in tortoise formation, covering themselves with their shields (facing page)

IRISH CHARIOTS are frequently mentioned in mythology

or even across the sea to Britain on giant slave raids. Sometimes groups of young men would form their own mercenary bands called Fianna and sell their services to the kings.

With Celtic society's emphasis on martial ability, warriors came to prize one-on-one combat above all else. Thus the Celts generally fought without strategy or tactics. Most Celtic battles probably consisted of two mobs of warriors rushing towards one another

and quickly pairing off into individual combats.

Celts in other parts of Europe employed a number of horsemen in their armies, but it is difficult to say how common this was in Ireland. The same is true of chariots. Although Irish myth often speaks of chariots, and they were certainly common in Britain, no archaeological evidence of their use has ever been discovered in Ireland.

While the Celts were fearsome warriors, their individual approach to warfare made them vulnerable to organised opponents. Since the Romans failed to reach Ireland, the Celts never faced their highly organised armies, and thus never needed to adopt their way of fighting. Although the Vikings would eventually bring superior weapons technology to Ireland, it wasn't until the coming of the Normans that the flaw in the Celtic way of warfare would be fully revealed.

St. Patrick

In a time of chaos and violence, St. Patrick led a mission to Ireland that would forever change the country's religion, culture and people.

Sometime in the fifth century, St. Patrick set quill to parchment and composed his *Confession*, possibly the first written work in the history of Ireland. He wrote in defence of himself and the churches he had built. He wrote to praise God and thank him for his guidance. *The Confession* reveals much about the life of Ireland's patron saint.

ST. PATRICK
led a mission to
Ireland to spread
Christianity

St. Patrick was born in the north of Britain around the end of the fourth century (some scholars give his date of birth as 387 AD) with the Roman name, Patricius. But those were the dying days of Roman rule in Britain, and the coastal defences had crumbled. Irish raiders plagued the western shore. When he was 16 years old, Patrick was kidnapped and taken to Ireland as a slave, possibly in one of the great raids led by Niall of the Nine Hostages.

For six years, Patrick toiled as a herdsman in the north of Ireland. He slept in the cold and often suffered from hunger pangs. In his misery, the formerly unreligious Patrick turned to God, praying many times a day. Then one night, he heard the voice of God telling him that a ship waited to take him home. Patrick escaped from his master and journeyed 200 miles to reach the ship.

In his *Confession*, Patrick says little about the years after his escape, just that his family welcomed him home. Many stories and legends state that Patrick later travelled to Gaul, where he studied in the monasteries. However, Patrick claimed to be an uneducated man, who had missed his chance at education.

NORTH OF IRELAND
where St. Patrick worked as a herdsman

Wherever he resided, Patrick heard the voice of God once more, telling him to return to Ireland to spread his word.

Patrick spent years travelling around the north, preaching to the pagan Irish. He built numerous churches, including the one that served as his base in Armagh. In one story, Patrick is said to have grabbed a

CHRISTIAN SETTLEMENTS

St. Patrick, driving out the snakes from Ireland

Patrick was not the first Christian to venture to Ireland. In fact, many small Christian settlements already existed, and the Pope had already sent one bishop to try and organise the Irish church. But the arrival of St. Patrick heralded a great change in the island. According to legend, when Patrick came to Ireland he drove out all the snakes. In all likelihood, Ireland never had any snakes, but the story is probably metaphorical. The snakes may have represented the druids, whose pagan beliefs connected them with Satan, the serpent in the Bible's book of Genesis.

handful of shamrocks in an attempt to explain the Holy Trinity and thus gave to Ireland its national symbol.

By the time Patrick wrote his *Confession*, his church was well established. Patrick appointed many bishops in Ireland, and they continued to lead the church after his death. Within a few centuries of his mission, most of Ireland had converted to Christianity, although many pagan traditions still survived. In the twelfth century, St. Patrick's remains were 'discovered' at Lough Derg, where Patrick had reportedly fasted in order to expel demons. With its unique focus on penitence, the site remains an important and popular pilgrimage destination.

Although born in Britain, St. Patrick is perhaps the most important figure in Irish history. His mission had a profound effect on the Irish national identity that still exists today. As such, St. Patrick's Day is one of the most celebrated days in the Irish calendar.

ST. PATRICK'S GRAVE at Downpatrick in Northern Ireland

The Monasteries

Established as religious focal points for Gaelic Christianity, the Irish monasteries expanded into unrivalled centres of art and learning.

IRISH MONKS
spent hundreds of hours copying books by hand

During St. Patrick's lifetime or soon after, other Christians arrived on the island from Britain and mainland Europe to preach the Gospel to the pagan Gaels. Within two centuries the new religion had replaced paganism as the dominant belief system. Along with Christianity came a new form of societal structure, the monastery.

Soon after their establishment, the monasteries became the largest settlements in Ireland. They normally consisted of a small church, surrounded by numerous wooden houses, barns and meeting halls, often enclosed by a wall or palisade. They resembled towns, but functioned more like modern universities.

As most of Western Europe sank into a dark age, following the collapse of the Western Roman Empire, Ireland saw an explosion of thought and learning.

IRISH CULTURE

Since Christianity came to Ireland peacefully, the Irish culture had time to adapt to this new religion while keeping a sense of Gaelic individuality. The Gaelic arts found new expression within the context of Christianity. In the monasteries, artists produced stone-carved Celtic crosses, intricate metal-work on chalices and shrines, and glorious illuminated manuscripts, such as the world-famous Book of Kells. This ninth-century collection of the gospels now resides on permanent display in Trinity College, Dublin, as a testament to the merging of Irish faith and art.

THE BOOK OF KELLS demonstrates the fusion of Irish faith and artwork (previous page and below)

With the arrival of Christianity came Latin, the first true written language in Ireland. The Gaelic Celts already had an established oral tradition of history, poetry and legal structures. So, while monks copied ancient Latin religious texts, laymen adapted Latin characters to the Irish language to produce the first written Irish works. The libraries in the Irish monasteries were some of the most extensive of their day, containing works on a variety of subjects.

Irish monasteries included numerous lay people who produced the best examples of Irish art, music, poetry, history and law. The most famous of the monasteries, such as Armagh, Kildare, Clonard and Clonmacnoise, became famous throughout Europe. When the Scandinavian warriors known as Vikings raided Ireland, the monasteries became targets, not only for their wealth, in the form of worked gold and other metals, but for the people who could be sold as slaves by the invaders. The Vikings came, sacked and burned the monasteries to the ground. However, the Irish rebuilt the monasteries, ensuring their survival.

IRISH MONASTERIES
often built towers to keep a look-out for attacks from Vikings or other Irish

Eventually, the Norman invasion brought an end to the monasteries. The Normans built castles which became centres of local government and commerce. They stripped the wealth from the monasteries and hired away the artisans. For many, the age of the monasteries was the golden age of Ireland, where the expression of Gaelic culture reached its peak.

The Early Irish Saints

After the collapse of the Roman Empire, the early Irish saints founded a monastic tradition that helped preserve Western Christian culture.

MAP OF WALES
where many of the early Irish Saints studied before returning to Ireland

While St. Patrick stands above all other figures in the history of the early Irish Church, he was only the first link in a chain of saints and churchmen that turned Ireland into a cultural haven amidst the violence and chaos of the dark ages. One of the most important of these early church figures was St. Finnian of Clonard.

Thought to have been born around 470 AD, St. Finnian spent most of his early life in Wales studying under the great saints there. Around 510 AD, he returned to Ireland and travelled the country preaching, teaching and founding

ST. COLUMBA

As a young man, Columba argued with one of the other Twelve Apostles of Ireland, and the argument led to a battle in which many men were killed. To atone for this sin Columba exiled himself to Scotland and set up a monastery on the island of Iona. From this base, he led Christian missions to the Picts (the inhabitants of Scotland at the time). Iona became the main centre of learning in Scotland, and Columba became famed as a missionary, scholar and diplomat. From Iona, his churches and monasteries spread across the Scottish islands.

St. Columba (c521–597 AD) preaching

churches. Finally, it is said that an angel led him to Clonard (or Cluain Eraird) where he built a church and settled down to a life of study and prayer. But his fame soon attracted attention, and holy men travelled from far and wide to study under him. Eventually over 3,000 men studied under Finnian at Clonard.

ST. COLUMBANUS

St. Columbanus
(c540–615 AD)

The tradition of St. Columba's monastic mission would soon be picked up by the similarly named St. Columbanus. Born around 540 AD, Columbanus spent much of his early life studying at the monastery in Bangor. Around the age of 40, he heard the voice of God calling him to preach his word in faraway lands. Setting out with twelve companions, Columbanus crossed over to Britain and from there into Gaul. The group quickly became famous in Gaul for their wisdom and piety. They settled in Burgundy and spent the next twenty years teaching, healing and founding monasteries. Eventually, after a dispute with local churchmen and royalty, Columbanus left Gaul and travelled through modern Switzerland into Italy, where he continued his monastic work.

Finnian's greatest accomplishment was the teaching of the Twelve Apostles of Ireland, a collection of Irish saints who spread Finnian's monastic ideas across the whole of Ireland. Probably the best documented of the twelve was St. Columba of Iona (see previous page).

Because of the work of the early Irish saints, some scholars have argued that Ireland saved western culture. While this claim is probably more than a little overstated, it is certainly true that the founding of the monastic tradition played a large role in preserving the knowledge and traditions of the early church. Also, because of the works of saints such as Columba and Columbanus these traditions were reintroduced to many places within Europe.

ST. BRENDAN THE NAVIGATOR

Perhaps the most famous of the Twelve Apostles of Ireland was St. Brendan the Navigator. While most of his stories are more legend than history, they reflect the idea of monastic exploration prevalent in Ireland at the time. Among Brendan's many adventures is landing on an island that turns out to be a sea monster, encountering pig-headed people with wolf legs and, of course, the discovery of America.

St. Brendan (c484–577 AD)

The Vikings

Best remembered for their viciousness and cruelty, the Vikings also brought important societal changes to Ireland.

VIKING LONGSHIPS were often called 'dragon ships' because of the dragon heads carved into their prows

In 795 AD the Vikings descended upon Ireland. Crossing the seas in their dragon-headed longships, these Scandinavian pirates attacked monasteries and isolated settlements, burning, looting and pillaging in search of gold and treasure. Those they did not kill, they took captive to be sold as slaves. For nearly 35 years they launched amphibious assaults all around the coast of Ireland. But the worst was yet to come.

Around the year 830 AD, the small Viking raids were replaced by vast assault fleets. Forces of 50 ships or more appeared at the mouths of Ireland's great rivers. The shallow draft of their ships allowed the Vikings to row into the interior, sacking the great monasteries, such as Clonmacnoise and Clonfert. Within a decade, these invaders began to build permanent bases in Ireland. These fortified harbours, called *longphorts*, allowed them to protect their ships and ride out the cold and dangerous winters that made sailing risky.

Over time, the *longphorts* became the first true towns in Ireland. Where the monasteries had been centres of learning and culture, the Viking towns became places of trade and commerce. The Vikings were master sailors and traders, and soon goods from all over Europe made their way into the Viking towns of Dublin, Limerick and Cork. The Vikings also brought with them advanced techniques for shipbuilding, farming and local government. It was in these towns that the first Irish coins were minted.

VIKING RAIDS became common in Ireland during the ninth and tenth centuries

Despite their military power and wealth, the Vikings never attempted to conquer the entire island. Content in their established towns and bases, they were perhaps more interested in establishing kingdoms in Britain.

VIKING RUNES
were part of a highly developed language

IRISH POWER STRUGGLES

With the establishment of settlements, the Vikings quickly became embroiled in Irish power struggles, representing just one more player in the never-ending cycle of conflicts among the various Irish kingdoms. At this time, the Irish had no sense of national unity, and were just as likely to ally with various Viking groups as with other Irish to fight their enemies. It was not long before the Irish noble families began to intermarry with the Vikings to form alliances. However, the great wealth of the Viking towns made them tempting targets for many of the Irish kings. Dublin was sacked and burned on more than one occasion. In 968 AD, Mathgamain, the king of the Dál Cais tribe, famously attacked and looted Limerick, making off with jewels, saddles and beautifully woven cloth.

THE VIKINGS
carved runic characters into stone

VIKING TOWNS
were the first true
towns in Ireland

By the end of the tenth century, Viking power was on the wane. Although they held several strategic towns, the great fleets were no longer sailing from Scandinavia and Irish rulers increasingly sought to bring the Viking towns under their power. In 1014, a large Viking army was defeated at the battle of Clontarf, an event often used to mark the end of the Viking era in Ireland.

Although the true Irish legacy of the Vikings was their establishment of the great coastal towns that would grow to be major cities, it is their image as vicious raiders from the sea that has captured the popular imagination.

Brian Bórú and the Battle of Clontarf

Brian Bórú, famed as a warrior and a statesman, became High King of Ireland and has passed into legend as the greatest Irishman of them all.

THE RIVER SHANNON flowed through the ancient kingdom of Dál Cais

In the midst of the Viking wars a new power arose among the Irish. Inside the territory of Munster, the small kingdom of Dál Cais sat astride the strategically important river Shannon and slowly expanded its borders through war and politics. Sometime after 950 AD, the crown of Dál Cais passed to Mathgamain who battled against both the Irish and the Vikings to make Dál Cais the most powerful kingdom in Munster. But in 976 AD, Mathgamain was assassinated, and the kingship passed to his brother, Brian.

King Brian Bórú hunted down his brother's killers, slaughtering one group in a church and defeating others on the battlefield. Once his family was avenged, Brian suppressed all opposition within Munster and

BRIAN BÓRÚ
(941–1014)
is regarded as
the greatest of the
ancient Irish kings

pushed northwards. Soon his forces began to clash with those of Máel Sechnaill II, the High King of the Uí Néill tribe. For years, the two great kings struggled against one another. Then in 997 AD, Brian and Máel Sechnaill met and agreed to split Ireland between them. Two years later they fought side-by-side on the battlefield of Glen Máma in Wicklow and together defeated Sitric Silkenbeard, King of the Dublin Vikings.

However, the alliance could not survive Brian's ambitions, and through political manoeuvering, Brian forced Máel Sechnaill to submit and to acknowledge him as High King of Ireland in 1002. Brian thus became the first king outside of the Uí Néill to claim lordship over the whole of Ireland. For the next ten years, Brian travelled the length of Ireland consolidating his position. During this time he also increased his influence within the Irish church by obtaining positions of power for his relatives and through generous donations of gold. For a brief time, Ireland was nearly united under a strong and determined ruler. That ended in 1014 at the battle of Clontarf.

Unravelling the true facts about the battle is fraught with difficulties, as sources are unreliable, but by looking at all of the available sources, some sort of narrative can be discerned.

In 1013, Máel Mórda, the King of Leinster, revolted and allied himself with Brian's old adversary, Sitric Silkenbeard. Now at least seventy years old, Brian rallied his forces and marched to Dublin where Máel Sechnaill joined him. For months they besieged the Viking fortress town, allowing time for Sitric to send

BATTLE OF CLONTARF
ended with the Irish chasing the Vikings into the sea

for help. Viking warriors arrived from all over the British Isles and possibly beyond. Then, Máel Sechnaill abandoned the siege, leaving Brian on his own.

THE BATTLE OF CLONTARF

On Good Friday in 1014, Máel Mórda led his Leinstermen and the Vikings on to the field near Dublin. They drew up in a long battleline opposite the forces of Munster, who were led by Brian Bórú's son Murchad. Brian himself stood to one side, his strength gone with age. All day the two armies clashed and many fell on both sides including Murchad and Máel Mórda. As the sun waned, the Vikings broke and the men of Munster slaughtered them without mercy. But the victory was marked with a final tragedy. As one Viking fled the field, he stumbled across Brian's tent and found the king unguarded. With his axe, he split the old king's head. The death of Brian Bórú marked the birth of his legend, and over the ensuing centuries that legend has often overshadowed the historical man. Dozens of stories and feats of arms have been attributed to him, and even his name, Bórú (or Bóruma) may be a later addition. Meanwhile his fatal victory at Clontarf has come to symbolise the Irish spirit of resistance and a willingness to sacrifice everything in the name of Ireland. In legend, perhaps even more than life, Brian Bórú is the High King of Ireland.

VIKING AXE
A heavy weapon that could smash through armour

The Norman Invasion

The Norman Invasion caused over eight centuries of English involvement in the governing of Ireland.

After the death of Brian Bórú, the political unity of Ireland crumbled. The title of High King became an empty honour, and Ireland reverted to a state of near constant warfare between the various territorial kings. Into this power struggle came Diarmait Mac Murchada, whose name now lives in infamy in the hearts of Irishmen.

In the middle of the twelfth century, Diarmait Mac Murchada succeeded to the kingship of Leinster. In 1152, Diarmait kidnapped the wife of one of his rivals, Tigernán, king of Bréifne. Although his wife was returned unharmed, Tigernán fostered a grudge against the Leinsterman. Nearly 15 years later, Tigernán and his allies drove Diarmait out of Leinster and out of Ireland.

THE LEINSTER REGION
although the ancient kingdom was probably much smaller

HENRY II (1133-1189) was the first English king to set foot in Ireland

In a decision that would have drastic consequences for the future of the island, Diarmait sought aid from Henry II, King of England. In 1167, Henry II was fighting in Aquitaine, France. Unable to spare any men, he authorised Diarmait to recruit allies from among his Anglo-Norman nobility in exchange for his fealty. Diarmait secured help from Richard Fitzgilbert de Clare, known as Richard Strongbow, and a group of his kinsmen collectively called the Geraldines.

Over the next few years, Diarmait and his Norman allies invaded Ireland in little waves. Diarmait recaptured his kingdom of Leinster but set his sights on the High Kingship. To bolster

THE MARRIAGE
of Strongbow and Aífe

his alliance with the Normans, Diarmait offered his daughter Aífe in marriage to Richard Strongbow. Now allied by family ties, Diarmait and the Normans marched on Dublin and captured the city. Then, in 1171, Diarmait died. By Irish law, the kingdom of Leinster could not pass to Strongbow as succession could not pass through the female line, nor could it pass to a foreigner. But Richard soon overcame opposition and took control of the kingdom.

Noting Strongbow's success, Henry recalled him to England, where Henry confirmed Richard as the Lord of Leinster, but claimed Dublin and some other territories for himself. He then organised a vast expedition to Ireland. Henry justified this invasion with a Papal letter known as *Laudabiliter*, whereby the Pope granted Henry the right to rule Ireland in order to reform the Irish church. When Henry's powerful army landed, many of the Irish kings came and submitted to him.

This invasion was really just a show of force and when Henry left, Ireland remained much the same as before. Several years after he returned to England, Henry granted lordship of all of Ireland to his youngest son, John. In 1185 Prince John travelled to Ireland and soon alienated most of the population. He took land from many loyal Irish and gave it to his allies. It is even said that some of his courtiers pulled upon the long beards of the Irish chieftains to see if they were real. It was an insult that would not be soon forgotten.

KING JOHN (1166-1216) was the first English king to also be 'Lord of Ireland'

When King Richard died in 1199, John became King of England and Lord of Ireland — the first to bear such a title. Although most of Ireland was still under the control of local leaders, the over-lordship of Ireland had been lost to the Irish. It would be seven centuries before it was even partially recovered.

A Time of Mercenaries: Gallowglass and Kerns

NORMAN HORSEMEN
were the premier
warriors of their day

After the initial conquests by the Norman invaders, the Irish hired professional soldiers from home and abroad in order to fight back.

Despite their conversion to Christianity, the Gaelic Irish maintained a proud warrior culture that prized individual strength and martial ability. However, by the twelfth century, they had fallen woefully behind the rest of Europe in terms of military development. Warfare between Irish factions had changed little in nearly a millennium. Irish armies still fought as disorganised mobs with individual heroics. Their warriors went into battle armed with swords and spears, but wearing little or no armour. When the Normans arrived, the Irish had no answer for their military advances.

THE NORMAN WARRIORS

The Normans were the foremost warriors of their day. Descended from Vikings, they had already seized kingdoms in both England and Sicily before they came to Ireland. The Normans fought in close formation where individual soldiers could lend support and protection to their fellows. They used bows and crossbows to unleash volleys of arrows that rained down upon enemy ranks. Most importantly, the Normans employed heavy cavalry. These knights wore chainmail armour, wielded long lances, and sat atop powerful warhorses. The strength and power of the cavalry charge allowed knights to plough through disorganised infantry as easily as a bulldozer. Within a few decades of their arrival, the Norman adventurers had seized direct control of most of the south eastern half of the country, an amazing feat considering that, apart from Henry II's brief expedition, the Normans in Ireland never numbered more than 3,000 fighting men.

A crossbow

A strongbow

With the Irish retreating on all fronts, the Gaels eventually turned to *gallóglach* or 'foriegn warriors' from Scotland. These mercenaries, who eventually became known as gallowglass, turned the tide in the ongoing struggle. The first gallowglass came from the western islands of Scotland, and served as the elite

GALLOWGLASS
warriors first came to Ireland from Scotland to serve as elite bodyguards

NORMAN WARRIORS
generally wore heavy armour and carried large shields

bodyguard of Irish kings and princes. Once they had proved their prowess in fighting the Normans, they were hired in greater numbers. Gallowglass fought on foot, encased in heavy armour. They carried battleaxes and two-handed swords that could tear through chain-mail and sever the legs of warhorses. Professional warriors, the gallowglass could stand up to the Normans on the battlefield.

With the English kings of the time seemingly disinterested in Ireland, the island once again descended into a chaotic cycle of petty wars between

Irish chieftains and Norman adventurers. Both sides soon realised that large, heavily-armed forces were often ill-suited to this type of warfare, and instead they turned to the kerns. These groups of lightly-armed, native Irish warriors roamed the island looking for employment. Lords on both sides hired them to raid their enemies' lands and to bolster the size of their armies. When they could not find work, the kerns often turned to banditry. While under employment, kerns were often charged with collecting their own fees from the local workforce. Thus, unsurprisingly, many kerns became little better than extortionists, preying on the population they were supposed to be protecting.

BATTLE AXES enabled the gallowglass to fight against heavily armoured Normans

Although both the gallowglass and the kerns developed to meet the needs of Irish warfare in the post-Norman invasion period, their success ensured that they would continue to form the basis of all Irish and, later, Anglo-Irish armies for centuries to come. However, especially in the case of the kerns, they also added to the general lawlessness and violence that permeated Ireland at the time.

Edward and Robert the Bruce

In a desperate bid to free themselves from their Anglo-Norman overlords, the Irish turned to the Scottish for help. The result was a disaster.

EDWARD I (1239–1307) spent most of his reign fighting the Welsh and the Scots and generally ignored Ireland

During the reign of Edward I (1272–1307) the chaotic and violent political situation in Ireland deteriorated even further. In the early years of his kingship, the strong and charismatic Edward ignored Ireland almost completely and focused on the conquest and suppression of the Welsh. However, during the last decade of the thirteenth century, Edward became embroiled in a bitter and costly war with the Scots. In need of funds, Edward sent Sir John Wogan to Ireland with orders to raise soldiers and money. Wogan proved to be ruthlessly and destructively efficient. In five years, he gathered thousands of Irish troops and sent them off to fight in the Scottish wars, all at the expense of Ireland. When Edward I died in 1307, he left behind a weak king on the throne, an unfinished war with Scotland and a virtually bankrupt Ireland.

Edward II did his best to rectify the damage done to Ireland by his father, but it was too little, too late. When King of the Scots, Robert the Bruce, led his army to victory at the battle of Bannockburn in 1314, he set an example of a Celtic country defeating the English. Later that year, the Irish of Ulster called upon Robert's brother, Edward Bruce, to come and take up the kingship of Ireland. In 1315, Edward Bruce set sail with a force of 200 ships and landed in Northern Ireland.

Backed with a large army and huge popular support in Ulster, Edward Bruce quickly took control of Ulster and Connacht. In Meath,

ROBERT THE BRUCE (1274–1329) (facing page) is commemorated by a statue at Stirling

EDWARD II (1284–1327) was a weak and ineffectual king who did his best to bring stability to Ireland

THE REMONSTRANCE

In Ulster, Edward Bruce was met by Domhnall Ó Néill, who granted to him the High Kingship of Ireland, based on his own weak claim through descent. Around the same time, Domhnall sent his famous Remonstrance to the Pope. This letter explained why Domhnall had sided with Edward Bruce, and outlined the various depredations that the Irish had suffered under English rule. In it, he stated that the Irish were given no standing in English law and that any Englishman could kill an Irishman without fear of punishment. Although the political effects of the Remonstrance were minimal, the letter has been passed down through history as an important document in the ongoing struggle between the Irish and the English.

he defeated the English magnate, Roger Mortimer, Lord of Trim, and continued to march south. On the verge of achieving total victory, nature intervened against Edward Bruce. In those years, a terrible famine swept across Europe and by 1316 it had ravaged Ireland. Unable to sustain his army on the march, Edward retreated back to the north, setting up his headquarters in Carrickfergus Castle. He then returned to Scotland and convinced his brother Robert to come and fight with him.

Together the brothers campaigned in Ireland and achieved a string of victories. But their army was forced to live off the land, taking food from the already famine-deprived Irish. The Scots soon lost popular support and once again retreated north. Robert returned to Scotland while Edward remained in Ireland.

CARRICKFERGUS CASTLE served as Edward Bruce's base while in Ireland

By the time Edward marched forth again in 1318, opportunity had passed him by. The Irish people had abandoned the Scots, considering them to be even more unfavourable than the English. To make matters worse, Edward II had finally sent money from England to organise an effective resistance. On the battlefield of Faughart, in what became known as the Battle of Dundalk, Edward Bruce died and with him went any dreams of a unified Celtic front against the English.

The Statutes of Kilkenny and the English Pale

The fourteenth and fifteenth centuries saw the people of Ireland break into three social groups: the Gaelic Irish, the Anglo-Irish and the English.

EDWARD III (1312–1377)
sent his son Lionel to try to regain control over Ireland

Ravaged by the Scottish invasion and the famine of the early fourteenth century, Ireland was left a wasted and depopulated land. The central English government collapsed, unable to enforce laws, raise revenue, or even provide more than a token defence. Ireland once again became wild and lawless. Part of the problem for the English in Ireland came from absentees. These were powerful English nobleman who owned vast territory in Ireland in addition to lands held in England. Almost without exception, these nobles preferred to live on their English estates and often paid little attention to what happened on their Irish lands.

The most powerful absentee was Lionel, Duke of Clarence, Earl of Ulster, and son of King Edward III.

In 1361, Edward III sent his son to Ireland to reclaim his Earldom from the Irish, and to re-establish royal authority. For five years, Lionel campaigned in Ireland, but failed to improve the situation. He blamed this partly on the Anglo-Irish barons, who had been reluctant to help. As his last act before leaving, Lionel summoned an English parliament, which passed the infamous Statutes of Kilkenny.

JERPOINT ABBEY
Cloisters at Jerpoint Abbey, Kilkenny, Ireland

The Statutes of Kilkenny remain a hotly debated topic among historians. Some see them as an attempt by an isolated colony to maintain its cultural identity against a huge majority. Others condemn them as codified racism designed to destroy Gaelic society. Among the 36 clauses in the statutes were

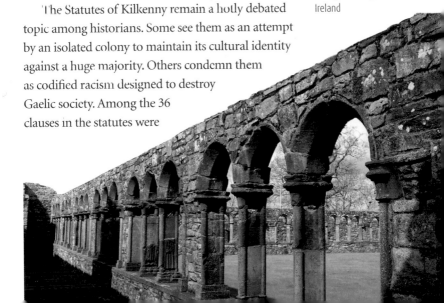

THE THREE SOCIAL GROUPS

At this time, the people of Ireland were divided into three distinct groups. The first was the Gaelic Irish, the descendants of the ancient Celts. The second was the Anglo-Irish, formed from the Irish who had intermarried with the original Norman invaders. This group contained many of the powerful lords of Ireland who adopted many aspects of both the English and the Irish culture. The final group was made up of the newly arrived English, mostly warriors and artisans who tended to stay in the areas around Dublin.

HURLING
was outlawed
under the Statutes
of Kilkenny

laws prohibiting the English from marrying the Irish, speaking the Irish language, or employing Irish bards. Even the popular sport of hurling was outlawed. Other statutes forbade selling arms and armour to the Irish or hiring Irish kerns.

Whatever the ultimate aims of the statutes, they brought about little immediate change. The English lacked the ability to enforce the laws, and the Anglo-Irish barons ignored them. Only later, when the English

regained power, did the statutes become a useful tool for the English kings to use against their enemies in Ireland.

The petty wars continued, and as the generations passed, the Anglo-Irish barons became ever more Gaelicised and more powerful. Meanwhile the English colonists and settlers retreated against the chaos. By the fifteenth century, English authority only truly existed in the four counties around Dublin. This area became known as the English Pale – 'pale' being a medieval term for an area guarded by a series of fortifications. Confined within the Pale, the English stood on the edge of crisis. Unsupported by the English crown, a concerted effort by the Irish could have easily wiped them out. However, caught up in their endless feuds, the Irish could never organise that final blow. This failure would eventually cost the native Irish their freedom.

THE ENGLISH PALE
The map below depicts the area which became known as the English Pale

The Kildares

The Kildares dominated Irish politics for over sixty years and unwittingly helped bring about the domination of Ireland by the English crown.

As the second half of the fifteenth century dawned over Ireland, the people of the island remained divided into their three distinct social groups. Although these were not necessarily political distinctions and groups from different societies often allied with one another, the divide between the groups remained an impediment to the unification of Ireland. This changed with the rise to power of the Earls of Kildare.

The Earls of Kildare descended from the Geraldines who were among the first Normans to invade Ireland. However, like most of the Anglo-Irish, the descendants of the Geraldines spent the ensuing centuries adopting and adapting many of the customs of the native Irish. From positions of power, they made numerous alliances with the Irish chieftains and intermarried with Irish families.

TUDOR ROSE
was the symbol
of England's royal
House of Tudor

As the confusion of the War of the Roses consumed England, the Earldom of Kildare passed to Gearóid Mór (or Gerald Fitzgerald), 8th Earl of Kildare, who would soon be called the 'Great Earl' by both the Irish and the English of the Pale. A well educated man who could speak Irish, English and Norman French, Gearóid Mór proved to be a master politician, diplomat and unifier. His family connections made him the perfect compromise candidate to gain support from all inhabitants of Ireland, and the English King made Gearóid his deputy in Ireland. For nearly 20 years Kildare ruled Ireland as king in all but name. He even supported failed rebellions against the English kings, but gained pardons because of his power. For the first time since the days of Brian Bórú, Ireland enjoyed a semblance of peace and unity.

HENRY VII (1457–1509) was one of the first English kings to exert his authority over Ireland

By 1485, the War of the Roses was ended and Henry VII was on the English throne. The king soon turned his eye to Ireland, and in 1494, Henry sent Sir Edward Poynings to replace the Earl of Kildare as his deputy.

DUBLIN CASTLE
under attack in the
sixteenth century

THE ENGLISH CROWN
was in constant
conflict with
Gearóid Óg

Backed by a thousand armed men, Poynings arrested Gearóid Mór. Poynings then called a parliament which drew up a document known as Poynings' Law, stating that all bills of the Irish parliament had to be approved by the King of England. With this safeguard in place, the King recalled Poynings and released Gearóid Mór. Henry VII saw that peace in Ireland depended on the Earl, so he reinstated him as his deputy. Despite his power, the Earl made no attempt to rebel against Henry. The Earl remained the figurehead of a somewhat unified Ireland, but the real power lay with the English king.

In 1523, Gearóid Mór died, leaving the Earldom to his son, Gearóid Óg. The new Earl increased the size of the family holdings, but came into constant conflict with the English crown. Three times the King appointed him deputy of Ireland, and three times the King had him arrested for various political reasons. Gearóid Óg was finally imprisoned in the Tower of London, leaving the running of his domains to his son, Lord Offaly.

History remembers Lord Offaly as 'Silken Thomas', a headstrong youth who would dress himself and his guards in fancy silks. During his father's arrest, Silken Thomas rode to the Irish Parliament to renounce his allegiance to the King, then led his men on a rampage through the English Pale. During his rebellion, Silken Thomas's men murdered the Archbishop of Dublin, John Alen; a crime which earned him excommunication by the Pope. Support for Silken Thomas melted away. Soon after, the English took him prisoner and eventually executed him.

SILKEN THOMAS (1513–1537) was executed at the Tower of London in 1537

Silken Thomas's rebellion came too late for Ireland. Had his grandfather, the Great Earl, led an uprising against the King it may well have been successful. Instead, the power of the Kildares had been broken, and Ireland now belonged to the King of England.

The Irish Reformation and the Catholic Reaction

With the advent of the Church of Ireland, King Henry VIII created a divide that would eventually tear the country apart.

After the defeat of the Kildares, King Henry VIII sought to extend his control by creating a Church of Ireland. In 1536 he arranged for a 'Reformation Parliament' in Dublin, which called for the dissolution (breaking up) of the monasteries and the recognition of the English King as the head of the Church of Ireland.

The first of these resolutions was passed mainly on the basis of greed. Both the English nobility and the senior churchmen who sat in parliament had long been envious of the wealth held by the monasteries, and saw their dissolution as a chance to acquire valuable land. Minor churchmen in the lower house of parliament who argued against the move were expelled. The resolution passed, and the ancient monasteries were

HENRY VIII (1491–1547) was the first King of England also to hold the official title of King of Ireland

destroyed. Although these monasteries were pale shadows of the cultural centres of old and had become corrupt political offices, their dissolution still came as a shock to many of the Irish.

The parliament then moved on to the creation of a Church of Ireland with the King of England as its head. Even the churchmen who had voted for the dissolution stood against this bill. But again, money ruled the day. Henry's supporters in parliament bribed a number of the bishops to switch sides, and the bill passed as the Act of Supremacy.

Four years later, in 1540, Henry VIII's new deputy in Ireland, Sir Anthony St. Leger, called another parliament and pushed through a bill declaring Henry to be King of Ireland. Previously, the English crown had only technically been 'Lord of Ireland'. Henry VIII viewed these parliaments as a complete success, recognising his authority in all

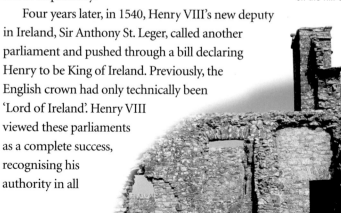

RUINS
of an Irish monastery
on the Hill of Slane

RESURGENCE OF THE CATHOLIC CHURCH

Henry VIII had little interest in the Irish population outside of the English Pale. There, the Catholic Church enjoyed a major resurgence. The monks who had been ejected from their monasteries and the majority of the priesthood who had remained loyal to Rome, preached the authority of the Catholic Church. Meanwhile, the Irish and many of the Anglo-Irish adhered to the Roman Church as a symbol of defiance. They pulled their children out of English schools and sent them to Catholic schools in Europe. A new generation of Irish joined the priesthood with the intention of keeping the Church alive in Ireland.

St. Peter's Basilica, Rome

matters of state and religion. But in the long term, the acts they imposed, specifically the Act of Supremacy, created a more unstable, anti-English population. Unwittingly, Henry VIII had created a link between the idea of religion and a newly forming Irish nationalism. He had gained the power he sought, but created a divide that haunts both the Irish and the English to this day.

Desmond's Rebellions and the Munster Plantation

The Desmond Rebellions and the Munster Plantation had limited impact, but were ominous precursors to the future of Ireland.

HENRY VIII
established the
Church of Ireland

Henry VIII achieved more than any of his predecessors in extending royal authority to Ireland. Through a system of 'Surrender and Re-grant', the King invited the Irish chieftains to surrender their lands to the crown and have them re-granted. The Irish received official

English titles and recognition under English law while becoming vassals of the monarch. Despite these gains, Henry still had little direct control over the affairs of those outside of the English Pale. Also, his establishment of the Church of Ireland had created a schism between the Irish and English that festered after his death as the crown eventually passed to the Catholic Mary, and then to her Protestant sister, Elizabeth.

Queen Elizabeth restored the monarchy as the head of the Church of England and Ireland, but adopted a less antagonistic approach to the affairs of religion, allowing the Irish to practise Catholicism freely. However, Elizabeth would accept no challenge to her authority, either through politics or religion, and often dealt harshly with those who defied her.

Meanwhile, Ireland continued to be ruled more by individual barons and chieftains than by any central authority. Cattle-raids, infighting, and assassination continued to be central parts of Irish politics.

QUEEN ELIZABETH I (1533-1603) allowed the Irish to practise Catholicism freely

Then, in the wake of Desmond's Rebellions, Elizabeth confiscated huge tracts of devastated, but still fertile land, in Munster. In order to make this land once again profitable, she organised the Munster Plantation.

LAND IN MUNSTER was confiscated by the Queen

Under this plan, English settlers were given a certain number of acres of land in return for rent to the Crown. Due to poor organisation and corruption, the plantation was never completely successful, and much of the land eventually reverted to the native Irish or to the Old English.

In the end, neither the Desmond Rebellions nor the Munster Plantation had a giant impact on the history of Ireland, but both incidents served as portents of bigger, more catastrophic events to come.

DESMOND'S FIRST REBELLION

In 1565, a feud between the Earl of Desmond and the Earl of Ormond resulted in a pitched battle at Affane. Elizabeth summoned both Earls to England. The Earl of Ormond she released, but the Earl of Desmond – an uneducated, uncultured and crippled man – aroused her suspicions. She had him locked in the Tower of London. When the news reached Ireland, the Earl's cousin, James Fitzmaurice Fitzgerald, organised an uprising against the Crown. Although limited mostly to the area of Munster, the rebellion ran for several years. The English besieged a number of renegade castles, slaughtering the inhabitants when they fell. The rebellion eventually petered out when the Queen released the Earl of Desmond, and Fitzmaurice went into exile.

DESMOND'S SECOND REBELLION

In 1579, Fitzmaurice returned to Ireland with a small band of followers proclaiming a holy war against the excommunicated Queen Elizabeth. Although Fitzmaurice was killed soon thereafter, others, including the Earl of Desmond, took up the cause. Queen Elizabeth sent a small army to Ireland, including heavy cannons that could destroy castle walls. The second Desmond rebellion proved a bloody affair. The English engaged in a scorched earth policy that devastated Munster. Crops were burnt and livestock slaughtered. All men of military age were deemed traitors and likely to be executed. Tens of thousands of people died of starvation. By the time Desmond was killed and the English army prevailed, Munster had been reduced to a smouldering ruin.

A detail from a woodcut plate, **The Image of Irelande** by John Derrick, 1581, depicting Desmond's second rebellion

Tyrone's Rebellion

Also called the Nine Years War, the rebellion of Hugh O'Neill, Earl of Tyrone, proved to be the last great uprising of the old Irish Chieftains.

Despite the various uprisings, such as Desmond's Rebellions, the reign of Queen Elizabeth I of England saw most of Ireland come more firmly under royal control. More Irish Chieftains submitted to Surrender and Re-grant, while the English administration which extended from the Pale became more self-sufficient. Once again, Ireland began to provide a revenue stream for the crown, and English adventurers came to the island to try and claim private holdings. As the sixteenth century drew to a close, only the region of Ulster remained mostly free from direct royal authority; mainly thanks to Hugh O'Neill, the Earl of Tyrone. In 1593, the tensions between the Irish in Ulster and the English adventurers broke into open conflict. For a time, Hugh O'Neill maintained a

QUEEN ELIZABETH I
saw most of Ireland come more firmly under royal control

HUGH O'NEILL

Hugh O'Neill was raised in an English household inside the Pale after the assassination of his father. A charming and intelligent youth, Hugh found favour among the English and formed many important political connections. In 1587, the crown recognised Hugh as the Second Earl of Tyrone, granting him large holdings in Ulster. The English saw O'Neill as the perfect candidate to keep the other Irish of Ulster in check, supporting him with money and arms, and never suspecting the double game he played.

Once safe within his own Earldom, Hugh O'Neill quickly adopted native Irish ways. He held his great courts and feasts outside of his castles and employed traditional Gaelic poets and musicians. More importantly, he began to create a secret army

The bulk of the army was formed of the traditional gallowglass and kerns, but O'Neill also purchased hundreds of handguns and trained his soldiers in their use. He cemented alliances with his neighbouring Irish lords, and sent secret messages to the Catholic King of Spain.

charade of being a loyal servant of the Crown, while manipulating the Irish uprising behind the scenes. However, after a couple of years, he dropped the deception and loosed his army upon the English. The Earl proved to be a master tactician. By utilising his knowledge of the terrain, and the natural abilities of his light infantry, he consistently led the English forces into ambushes, where he could defeat them with little risk. He would then ask for peace as a ploy to gain time to regroup and reorganise his forces.

In England, Queen Elizabeth grew worried about this new threat. She sent her long-time friend the Earl of Essex to Ireland with a large army. The campaign proved a miserable failure that lost Essex his status at court, and led directly to his own attempted rebellion and eventual execution. Meanwhile, Elizabeth sent another army of nearly 20,000 men to Ireland – one of the largest forces ever assembled on the island. Soon thereafter, a Spanish army also landed in Ireland.

For years, Hugh O'Neill had worked in secret to form an alliance with Catholic

KINSALE LANDING
The Spanish landing at Kinsale in 1601

Spain, and in 1601 4,000 Spanish soldiers landed in Kinsale. On the southern coast of Ireland, Kinsale was hundreds of miles from O'Neill's powerbase. Still, he marched his army southwards and, for the first time, met the English in an open battle. The Irish forces were defeated, and the Spanish slipped away.

After nine years of warfare and struggle, Hugh O'Neill's support evaporated. He surrendered to the English, fully expecting to be executed. However, in a quirk of fate, Queen Elizabeth died a few days before his surrender. Her successor, James I, proved merciful. He pardoned Hugh O'Neill and even allowed him to retain his Earldom. But the power of the Irish was broken and soon their last great chieftains would flee the island. As King James took the throne, he could truly be said to rule Ireland.

JAMES I (1566–1625) pardoned Hugh O'Neill and allowed him to retain his Earldom

The Flight of the Earls and the Ulster Plantation

The departure of the Earls of Tyrone and Tyrconnell remains a great mystery of Irish history, and led directly to the Ulster Plantation.

In the destruction of the Nine Years War, the great Irish lords of the north had been defeated by the military might of England. But, because of the mercy of James I, they had retained a great deal of their land and power. Then, on 4 September 1607, these champions of Gaelic nobility boarded a ship at Rathmullen and set sail for Spain. No one can say for sure why Hugh O'Neill, Earl of Tyrone, Rory O'Donnell, Earl of Tyrconnell and Cúchonnact Maguire, Lord of Fermanagh left Ireland, only that they seem to have done so in a hurry. Although they took with them as many members of their families as they

PHILIP OF SPAIN was involved in a diplomatic incident over the Flight of the Earls

could gather, O'Neill left behind a son and O'Donnell a pregnant wife.

Of course, there are many conspiracy theories surrounding the Flight of the Earls. Some state that the Earls were plotting with Spain when their plans were discovered. Others accuse the English lords in Ireland of planning their assassination. In all likelihood, both theories contain a grain of truth. Either way, the Earls' ship never arrived in Spain. Blown off course, the ship made landfall in Normandy and sparked a major diplomatic incident between England, France and Spain. France refused to extradite (release) the fugitives back to England and Spain washed her hands of the affair, claiming they had no connection to the Earls. Eventually, the former lords of Ireland were packed off to Rome, where they quietly lived out their days.

To the later Irish romantics, the Flight of the Earls is depicted as the final act of defiance of the Irish noble lines and the end of the Gaelic era in Ireland. However, to the Irish left behind in Ulster, the flight proved an unmitigated disaster. King James declared the Earls and

MAP OF EUROPE
The Earls' ship made landfall in Normandy

their companions traitors and confiscated their lands – nearly 500,000 acres. The English government then displaced large sections of the population, broke up the land and parcelled out small pieces in a move known as the Ulster Plantation.

In the long run, the Ulster Plantation can be seen as a partial success for the British. The land became more profitable, less rebellious and more Anglo-centric. Unfortunately, it also contributed greatly to the divide that would eventually split the country in two.

THE ULSTER PLANTATION saw many native Irish expelled from their homes and land

THE ULSTER PLANTATION

Although previous plantations had been attempted in Ireland, the scale and organisation of the Ulster Plantation was unprecedented. Under this system, the land was divided into lots of 1,000–2,000 acres and offered up for rent. English renters, or 'undertakers', received the best land and the cheapest rent, but had to settle a certain number of English families on the land. Similar deals were offered to the Scottish. Some of the land was offered to the Irish, but at much higher rent.

Initially, the plantation met with problems. Foremost, not enough English and Scottish settlers could be found for the new land. Thus many undertakers illegally employed Irish workers. Other undertakers became absentees, grabbing what profit they could from the land and then heading for home. In both cases, the British charged their Irish tenants exorbitant rents that slowly sucked them dry and forced many to become 'woodkerns', bandits and raiders who lived in the forests. At the same time as the Ulster Plantation, other Scottish settlements grew up in the north, in and around Antrim, and these proved more resilient and successful.

A map showing the Ulster Plantation

Black Tom Tyrant

Thomas Wentworth adopted the policy of 'Thorough' and the power of the Castle Chamber to make Ireland a more efficient state.

The Flight of the Earls in 1607 marked a shift in the political struggles in Ireland. The pure lines of Irish nobility were now virtually extinct and the Old English families became the ruling class of the Irish. They had adopted the Irish language and culture, and had remained Catholic when England converted to Protestantism. But now, even the Old English were under threat from the land-grabbing New English adventurers flocking to the Irish plantations.

The Old English sought 'Graces' from the king to protect their rights. These Graces included laws to guard property rights, the repeal of the Oath of Supremacy, that prevented Catholics from holding important positions, and the abolition of recusancy fines for not attending mass.

When Charles I came to the throne of Britain and

CHARLES I (1600–1649)
came to the throne of Britain and Ireland in 1625

Ireland in 1625, he inherited a war with Spain and saw a chance to raise revenue in Ireland. While hinting that he would authorise the Graces, Charles raised £120,000 from the Irish. But, instead of the Graces, the Irish received the toughest, most efficient and most hated deputy the country had ever known: Thomas Wentworth, soon to be known as 'Black Tom Tyrant'.

Wentworth arrived in Ireland in 1632 and immediately set in motion his 'Thorough' policy to put Ireland back on track. Thorough implied a ruthless attention to detail in all facets of government. To raise funds he set up new customs duties and made Ireland a part of the trans-Atlantic trade that had grown up over the last century. He also continued the policy of plantations by seizing land based on old royal claims and offering it up for rent.

THOMAS WENTWORTH (1593–1641) became known as 'Black Tom Tyrant' and was hated by the Irish

THE CASTLE CHAMBER was used by Wentworth to threaten and imprison his enemies

To accomplish his Thorough policies, Wentworth employed two main weapons. The first was the Irish Parliament, which he packed with loyal representatives who granted him all the powers and funds he needed. The other was the Castle Chamber.

In many ways, the absolute dictatorial power wielded by Wentworth was reflective of the attempts by Charles I to do the same in England and Scotland. But whereas Wentworth successfully browbeat the Irish into submission, Charles's failures led to crisis and civil war. As his last major act in

THE CASTLE CHAMBER

Thomas Wentworth quickly seized control of the Castle Chamber – a royal court that had been in place for nearly sixty years. Although the court had only ever been used to try serious matters of state such as treason, Wentworth employed the Castle Chamber as a quick fix to many of his problems by using it to threaten or imprison his enemies.

Ireland, Wentworth imposed 'The Black Oath' on the
Scots in Ireland, forcing them to break their religious
connections with Scotland. He then left the island with
an Irish army to march to the support of his King.

However, soon after his arrival in England,
Wentworth was arrested by the anti-royalist factions
of the English Parliament on charges of subverting
the laws of England and Ireland. All of Black Tom
Tyrant's enemies in both countries testified against
him. Despite Wentworth's loyalty to the crown,
Charles I demonstrated his personal and political
weakness and had
Wentworth executed
in 1641.

WENTWORTH'S
execution took place
at Tower Hill, London

The 1641 Rising and the Confederate Catholics of Ireland

In 1641, the increasing tensions between Catholics and Protestants exploded into violence and soon became entangled in the confusion of the English Civil War.

During the years that Thomas Wentworth served in Ireland, he managed to suppress the underlying religious tensions through his application of absolute power. When he departed in 1639, he left a gaping power vacuum that could not be filled. The English Parliament, which was now on the brink of war with King Charles I, appointed a weak, Puritan government in Ireland that made the problems worse. The Catholic Old English land owners who had fought a long political struggle to obtain the Graces, began to despair and plot rebellion as a means to their political ends.

In 1641, a group of Old English in Ulster formed a plan to take over Dublin Castle as part of a general show of force against the government. Although the plan was betrayed, the rising proceeded and quickly spun out of control. Instead of a political protest, the native Irish in Ulster seized the opportunity to strike out against their English landlords. Thousands of English settlers were murdered by roving bands of woodkerns and oppressed Irish workers. Thousands more were forced out of their homes, stripped naked and sent fleeing to the safety of the protected towns.

DURING THE 1641 Ulster Rebellion only the high walls of towns and cities protected the English and Scottish

By 1642, the rising had spread out of Ulster to most of the country, although the actual violence of the movement had decreased. Meanwhile, highly embellished tales of

slaughter and massacres reached England and forced the fractured government to react. A small Scottish army landed in Ulster and engaged in a prolonged and systematically violent campaign of suppression. More English troops were sent to Dublin, where the Irish Parliament made the profound mistake of barring all Catholics from the assembly. With many of the formerly loyal Old English landowners now disenfranchised (deprived of their vote), they cast in their lot with the rebels and formed the Confederate

OWEN ROE O'NEILL

The Confederate Catholics found a strong military leader in Owen Roe O'Neill, nephew of the great Hugh O'Neill, Earl of Tyrone. Owen had fought in the Thirty Years War in Central Europe and brought this experience with him to the battles in Ireland. He desperately led the Irish against the English and Scottish on the one hand, while attempting to hold the Confederation together on the other.

Catholics of Ireland. For nearly a decade, this loose organisation functioned as the de facto government for most of the island.

For a moment, the rising, now called the Confederate War, became a straight rebellion of the Irish Catholics against the English Protestants, who were led by the Earl of Ormond. Then, as the war increased in intensity, the Civil War (The War of the Three Kingdoms) broke out in England. While small, disorganised battles raged all over Ireland, the Earl of Ormond tried to negotiate a treaty with the Confederation and seek their support for the King. Although a peace was signed, disunity reigned on both sides. The English Protestants were divided between Royalist and Parliamentarian, while the Irish were split between Royalists and those loyal to the Roman Catholic Church.

In 1649, everything changed. The war in England ended with the execution of Charles I, and a new army landed in Ireland. At its head was one of the most reviled figures in Irish history, Oliver Cromwell.

OLIVER CROMWELL
was to become one
of the most reviled
figures in Irish history

Oliver Cromwell

Oliver Cromwell's actions at the sieges of Drogheda and Wexford earned him a place as one of the great villains of Irish history.

**OLIVER CROMWELL
(1599–1658)**
moved quickly on his
arrival in Ireland

When Oliver Cromwell came to Ireland in 1649, he had already proven himself one of the most capable English generals in history. He had joined the Parliamentarians in the English Civil War and served as a cavalry commander at many major battles. When Charles I surrendered in 1646, Cromwell was second-in-command of the New Model Army.

With the confusion and destruction of the Civil War, it took some time before the new English government could organise an effective response to the war in Ireland that had seen continuous fighting since the 1641 rebellion.

When Parliament finally authorised an expedition in 1649, it placed Cromwell in command of a force of 12,000 troops and a massive artillery train. At the time, this New Model Army, which had emerged from the fires of the English Civil War, was the best trained and organised army in Europe. No army in Ireland could hope to defeat such a force in the field.

Cromwell moved quickly upon his arrival in Ireland. Determined to prevent an alliance between the Royalists under the Earl of Ormond and the Irish under Owen Roe O'Neill, Cromwell marched his army to the fortress town of Drogheda on the heights above the mouth of the River Boyne. Inside the fortified town, Sir Arthur Aston led a royalist army of 2,000. He refused Cromwell's call to surrender, determined to hold out for as long as possible. For three days, Cromwell's artillery battered at the walls of

SIEGES USUALLY began with an artillery bombardment in order to create a breach in the walls

THE THIRTY YEARS war was one of the most bloody and destructive wars in human history

Drogheda, slowly chipping away at the stone. On the third day, a section of wall collapsed and a breach was opened. Oliver Cromwell ordered his army forward and they poured through the gap, overwhelming the defenders. But the soldiers of the New Model Army didn't stop with the enemy combatants; they ran amok through the town, killing everyone they came across. At one point, they chased a group into a church steeple, then burned the church down around them. As many as 3,500 people died inside the fractured walls of Drogheda.

Within the context of seventeenth-century Europe, which had only recently escaped the horrors of the Thirty Years War, Cromwell's actions at Drogheda were neither remarkable nor unlawful. Still, Cromwell would later feel the need to justify his actions by claiming it as just punishment for the crimes of the 1641 uprising, and noting that it prevented later bloodshed by convincing other fortified towns to surrender without a fight. Most Irish towns thereafter

WEXFORD

As the New Model Army came to the town of Wexford, Cromwell called upon the town to surrender. While the negotiations were underway, the town was betrayed by the fortress next to it, and the English soldiers stormed into the town. The soldiers murdered nearly 2,000 people in an obvious breach of the rules of warfare.

Wexford town, today

offered no resistance and were left unharmed, with the notable exception of Wexford.

The ravages of Cromwell's army, coupled with the death of Roe O'Neill, proved to be the undoing of Irish unity, and organised resistance to the English Parliamentary forces eventually collapsed. Cromwell left Ireland only nine months after he arrived, but in that time he wrote his own legacy in Irish blood. Yet, despite the destructiveness of his army, Cromwell's greatest crimes against the Irish were yet to come.

The Cromwellian Land Settlement

In order to repay the debt incurred by his military campaigns, in 1652 Oliver Cromwell engineered the greatest man-made population upheaval in the history of Ireland.

A STATUE OF CROMWELL can be found at the Houses of Parliament, London

Despite the bloody victories of Cromwell in Ireland in 1649, the Confederate War lasted for another three years. The occupying English army eventually numbered 30,000 men, an overwhelming force that finally brought the war to a close in 1652. Ireland had been crushed. Nearly one-third of the Catholic population had died in the fighting or the associated plague and famine. Houses had been burnt or abandoned. Crops went unplanted. In England, the victory was tempered by the massive expense of the campaign. Parliament owed £3.5 million to investors, money-lenders and soldiers, and possessed only one source of revenue to raise this cash – Irish land.

THE ACT OF SETTLEMENT

In 1652, the English Parliament, now led by Oliver Cromwell, passed the Act of Settlement. The first action of this draconian statute identified the leaders of the enemy, such as the Earl of Ormond. These men were declared traitors, their lives and land forfeit to England. All other landowners in Ireland were forced to prove their 'constant good affection' for the English Parliament, a task nearly impossible in a country where Catholics and Protestants had been at war before Parliament even took charge. Those who failed had their lands seized, while being granted a proportionally smaller holding in Connacht.

Oliver Cromwell

The new Puritan government in Ireland carried out a land resettlement with brutal, if somewhat haphazard, determination. In some counties, English soldiers scoured the countryside rounding up traitors and either executing them or forcing them on the long march to Connacht. In other places, Irishmen successfully hid in the hills or kept a low enough profile to be overlooked. Many followed the old tradition of the woodkerns and became bandits. For many, the resettlement proved to be a death march. Forced off their lands before the crops could be harvested, the Irish struggled against hunger to reach their new lands, only to arrive too late in the season to hope to plant crops in their new rocky land.

Despite its harshness, the Act of Settlement succeeded on two levels. Firstly, it repaid the debts owed by the English Parliament, and secondly, it pushed nearly all of the old, mostly Catholic, landowners into one far corner of the island. However, like all of the great plantation movements before it, the Act of Settlement failed in its final aim of replacing the majority Irish population with a new Protestant English one. While the wealthy English gentry were happy to take on large tracts of Irish land,

ROUNDHEAD SOLDIER
depicted in full
battle dress

CATHOLIC LANDOWNERS
were forced to the
north-west corner
of the island

English tradesmen and workers were not interested in resettlement. Why go to an island famous for its murderous upheavals and banditry, especially with the more lucrative and appealing prospect of the New World only an ocean-crossing away?

The settlement equally failed in its attempts to settle English soldiers. Over 30,000 soldiers were granted land in Ireland, but nearly two-thirds immediately sold their land to their officers or other land-barons. Of the remainder, most quickly went native. Forced by necessity to marry Irish women, these soldiers raised children with Irish as their first language.

In the end, the Act of Settlement produced a similar result to all attempts at Irish resettlement. A new class of wealthy Protestant English landowners floated atop an oppressed Catholic majority. Although the harsh, Puritanical regime died with Oliver Cromwell in 1658 and the restoration of Charles II in 1660, the damage had been done. The Cromwellian government had rewritten the demographics of Ireland to produce a society notable for its inequality and its instability.

DEATH MASK
of Oliver Cromwell

The Williamite War and the Battle of the Boyne

When the English government ousted James II in favour of his son-in-law William, the Catholic James Stuart chose to make his stand in Ireland.

**JAMES II
(1633–1701)**
appointed Richard
Talbot as his deputy
in Ireland

Following the Restoration of Charles II to the throne of England, Scotland and Ireland in 1660, a level of peace returned to Ireland. Charles II repealed some of the harsh Puritan laws and even granted back a small portion of the lands that had been taken from Catholics. He also appointed the tolerant Earl of Ormond as his deputy in Ireland. For the next twenty-five years Ireland was able to rebuild.

In 1685, Charles II died and his brother James, a devout Catholic, succeeded to the throne. The Irish population rejoiced at having their first Catholic monarch in over one hundred years. James appointed Richard Talbot as his deputy in Ireland, and Talbot set about making Ireland a safe Catholic stronghold for the King. Called 'Lying Dick Talbot' by the Protestant Irish, the new deputy purged the Irish army of Protestants, creating a new force loyal to James Stuart.

A year after James II's ascension, his English subjects began plotting to replace him with his son-in-law, the Protestant, William of Orange. In 1688,

WILLIAM III (1650–1702) quickly succeeded James II

JAMES II
in ceremonial
armour

CANNON
– a weapon widely
used at the Battle
of the Boyne

William landed in Devon, and the English population
rose up to support him. James II fled to France, where
Louis XIV saw a chance to strike at his old enemy
William of Orange (now William III of England).
He sent James to Ireland with a small French force.
In 1689, James and his small army came ashore at
Kinsale. The Williamite War had begun.

Richard Talbot had done his job well, and by the
time James arrived only a few places in the north of
Ireland held out in support of William, notably Derry
and Enniskillen. James Stuart marched to Derry with
30,000 soldiers and demanded its surrender. The
populace refused and James's Jacobite army settled
into a long siege. For 15 weeks the city held out, until
an English fleet fought its way through to relieve the
city. Faced with the loss at Derry and the defeat of
another Jacobite army at Enniskillen, James retreated
back towards Dublin.

In June of 1691, William III arrived in
northern Ireland at the head of the largest
invading army in Irish history. Consisting of

English, Dutch, Danish, German and French Huguenot soldiers and sporting a massive artillery train, William's army was joined by 1,000 loyal Irish troops on its march south towards Dublin. Meanwhile, James Stuart, with his army of around 25,000 Irish and French troops, decided to make his stand along the River Boyne, a few miles from Drogheda.

THE BATTLE OF THE BOYNE

The battle commenced on 1 July 1690, when William used his overwhelming artillery superiority to hammer the Jacobite army. The Williamites used this cover fire to help ford the river, while a diversionary attack on one side of the line drew off James's best troops. James, realising he had been out-manoeuvred, ordered a general retreat. William let his father-in-law go. Although the Battle of the Boyne was not militarily decisive, it heralded the end of the Jacobite cause. After the battle, William took Dublin and James once again fled to France. Although the war would drag on for another year, the title of King was no longer in doubt.

The Treaty of Limerick and the Penal Laws

The Williamite War ended with the Treaty of Limerick, which promised religious freedom to all Catholics. The Treaty would not be honoured.

PATRICK SARSFIELD (1660–1693)
fought bravely against the English

LIMERICK
where a peace treaty was signed in October 1691

After their defeat at the Battle of the Boyne, Ireland's Catholics fought more for their own freedom and land than they did for James Stuart. For over a year they held on, desperately trying to stop the slow advance of the English army. In July 1691, the Jacobites made a stand at Aughrim in County Galway. Despite their strong position, the English managed to flank their line, and nearly 7,000 Jacobites died in the ensuing rout. It was the bloodiest battle ever fought in Ireland.

With the Catholic Jacobite cause nearing

THE TREATY OF LIMERICK

The Treaty of Limerick contained three major clauses:

~ Irish Catholics would be granted the same religious freedom they had enjoyed under Charles II.

~ They could not be tried for treason or other crimes related to the war and were secured in their lands and possessions.

~ Any Jacobite soldiers who so wished could depart Ireland with their arms.

This last clause launched the flight of the famous 'Wild Geese' – 12,000 Irish soldiers who left Ireland to fight in foreign armies, never to return.

extinction, command passed from the dying Richard Talbot to Patrick Sarsfield, Earl of Lucan. Sarsfield gathered his remaining forces in Limerick, as the army and navy of England closed in around him. By organising a brave defence, Sarsfield convinced the English that Limerick could not be taken by assault. However, Sarsfield also realised that his position was hopeless. The two sides met in negotiation and on 3 October 1691 the war ended with the Treaty of Limerick.

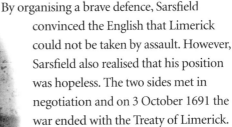

**QUEEN ANNE
(1655–1714)**
proved less tolerant
than William III

To King William III, the treaty seemed fair and the
end of the war a relief. However, his own Parliament and,
more importantly, the Protestant Parliament of Ireland,
saw it differently. Less than five years after the signing
of the treaty, the Irish Parliament began to pass laws
discriminating against Catholics, and to many Irish the
Treaty of Limerick became known as the 'Broken Treaty'.
Then, in 1702 the moderate King William III died after
falling from his horse and the monarchy passed to his
less tolerant sister-in-law Queen Anne.

For the next 30 years, the Irish Parliament passed
ever stricter laws against Catholics. Collectively known
as the 'Penal Laws', they were highly reminiscent of the
medieval Statutes of Kilkenny. Under the Penal Laws,
Catholics could not sit in Parliament nor serve as a
sheriff or member of a town council. They could not
join the army, own a gun or work as a lawyer or judge.
Catholics could not buy land or take out a lease for
more than 31 years. They could not send their children
to foreign schools, nor were Catholics allowed into
Trinity College.

Perhaps more importantly, the law stated that land owned by a Catholic must be divided equally amongst all his sons when he died, unless the eldest son converted to Protestantism; in which case he inherited everything. Even for families that remained Catholic and loyal to one another, the larger Catholic landholdings were slowly broken up into smaller and smaller pieces. Parliament never banned Catholicism outright, but it exiled all bishops, monks and friars. Priests were allowed to remain, but had to wear badges of office at all times, so they could be clearly identified. Finally, in 1728, Parliament passed the last of the Penal Laws, depriving all Catholics of the right to vote.

At the beginning of the eighteenth century, Catholics formed nearly 75 per cent of the Irish population, but it was a time of Protestant Ascendancy.

TRINITY COLLEGE
in Dublin did not accept Catholics

HEDGE SCHOOLS
where Catholic priests taught and held services

Jonathan Swift
(1667–1745)

Best known as the author of *Gulliver's Travels*, Jonathan Swift was also a noted propagandist and an unintentional father of Irish Nationalism.

JONATHAN SWIFT became an unintentional father of Irish Nationalism

At the beginning of the eighteenth century, Ireland entered a period known as the Protestant Ascendancy, most notable for the anti-Catholic Penal Laws enacted by the Irish Parliament. The effect of the Penal Laws on the population was devastating. Within a generation or two, Irish Catholics became one of the poorest classes of people in Europe. Many spent part of the year planting and harvesting crops, and the rest wandering the country begging for food. Even those that lived in little cottages possessed almost nothing. They slept on the ground, built fires in the dirt on the floor and cooked without utensils. The little money they earned mostly went to the landlords or to pay church tithes –

both to the Catholic Church, which was by choice, and the Church of Ireland, which was not.

While the members of the Protestant Ascendancy exploited the Catholic population, the Government in England exploited Ireland. The English Parliament had the right to block or enact any legislation in Ireland and used this power to suppress any industry that might have a detrimental effect upon the markets in England. However, when the English Parliament destroyed the Irish woollen industry by banning the export of Irish wool, they raised the ire of the Irish writer, Jonathan Swift.

Born in Dublin to an English father, Swift enjoyed many of the fruits of the Protestant Ascendancy. He received a good education and a position in the Church of Ireland. He served as a vicar, but he left Ireland for England as soon as he was able. In England he wrote propaganda for the government in the hope of obtaining an English bishopric. Instead, the church appointed him Dean

ENGLISH PARLIAMENT had a right to block or veto legislation in Ireland

ST. PATRICK'S
Cathedral in Dublin,
where Swift became
Dean

of St. Patrick's Cathedral in Dublin. From this position, Swift saw first-hand the devastation that the English Parliament had brought upon the Irish. Swift had little love for Ireland and even less for Catholicism, but the unnecessary cruelty of England fired his passions.

In 1720, Swift penned *A Proposal for the Universal Use of Irish Manufacture*, which called upon the Irish population to boycott all English products and only buy those manufactured in Ireland – a radical view for the time.

During 1724–25, Swift followed up *A Proposal* with a series of seven pamphlets known as the *Drapier's Letters* in which he attacked various English abuses and argued that Ireland should have the same right of government as possessed by the English Parliament. Swift became a hero in Ireland, even though the letters were signed M. B. Drapier. The furious government in England, unable to prove Swift's authorship of these seditious missives, arrested the printer. However, in a further embarrassment, no jury would convict the printer, and the case was dropped.

Several years later, after writing *Gulliver's Travels*, Jonathan Swift found time to pen one of the most disquieting and satirical political pieces in the history of the English language: *A Modest Proposal for Preventing the Children of Ireland from Being a Burden to their Parents or Country and for Making Them Beneficial to the Public.* In this tract Swift suggests that many of the problems of Ireland could be solved by eating poor children, 'stewed, roasted, baked or boiled', and even points out the side benefit of reducing the number of Papists.

If this last work seems in poor taste, it should be remembered that it was written with a venom inspired by the cruelty and injustice of a foreign government. Although Jonathan Swift was not a patriot, his writings helped to stir a sense of Irish nationalism that had never before existed. Perhaps for the first time in the history of Ireland, the people began to unite in the face of a common enemy.

GULLIVER'S TRAVELS (1726) became Swift's best known work. In it, Gulliver visits different lands, including one populated by giants

The Rise of Irish Nationalism and Prosperity

The second half of the eighteenth century proved to be a period of growth in Ireland, in industry, in population and in national identity.

In 1740, Ireland hit one of the lowest points in its often bleak and bloody history. Famine swept across Europe, and nowhere did it strike harder than amongst the

THE HUMBLE POTATO

Brought to Ireland in the sixteenth century, the humble, yet hardy, potato proved to be a near-perfect food for Ireland. Potatoes could grow in poor soil and just one acre planted with potatoes could provide food for a small family. With most Irish having only small pieces of land to manage, such a vegetable must have seemed a godsend. But the population grew too dependent on this one food source, and when the great frost destroyed most of the potato crop in 1740, they paid the price.

poor of Ireland. Part of the problem developed from the failure of Ireland's new staple crop, the potato.

However, out of the darkness came a spark of light. Unlike previous eras when famine had struck the country, this time Ireland had a better organised and more efficient social structure that could at least attempt to respond to the crisis. On New Year's Day in 1741, the Archbishop of Armagh began serving food to the hungry – thousands of people every day. His example was followed by others across the country. Even the English Viceroy, the Duke of Devonshire, lent a hand and supported a plan by the Charitable Music Society, which raised funds by inviting the composer George Frideric Handel to Ireland to premiere his newest work, *The Messiah*.

GEORGE FRIDERIC
Handel premiered his work, **The Messiah**, in Ireland in 1742

THE GREAT FROST
in the winter of 1740 destroyed most of the potato crop

**HENRY BOYLE
(1669–1725)**
led the Irish
Parliament

CATTLE FARMING
was important as
Ireland increased
trade and business

The famine of 1740–41 was probably the worst in the history of Ireland, and it is possible that nearly 500,000 people (or one fifth of the entire population) died. However, it is impossible to say how much worse it could have been if not for the charitable efforts of those in power.

From this point, Ireland began to heal and grow. The Penal Laws, which had suppressed so much of the population for so long, were slowly relaxed and repealed. New industry sprang up all over the island. The great forests of Ireland were stripped away, either for logging or to make room for cattle, or industry such as iron smelting. The government expanded the harbours in order to increase trade and continue to play an important role in trans-Atlantic shipping. A new, predominantly Catholic business class arose, as children who grew up under the Penal Laws strove forward in the one outlet left to them.

Yet, even as Ireland grew and expanded, the government in England did much to stymie its development. When the Irish linen and glass industries began to succeed, high tariffs and even outright bans on export were applied. When the Irish began to brew large quantities of beer successfully, England banned the Irish importation of hops, to keep English beers as the main drink. It was abuses such as these that Jonathan Swift had written about decades before, and now the people of Ireland were not going to surrender to them meekly.

In 1751, the Irish treasury found itself with a surplus, but Britain swooped in and claimed the money in the name of the King. When 1753 brought another surplus, the Irish Parliament, led by Henry Boyle, lobbied hard and retained the money. It was a huge victory for Ireland and prompted the birth of a new group in the Irish Parliament – the Patriots. The Patriots still had a long fight ahead of them to achieve their ultimate goal of parity with Britain under the rule of the monarch, but in 1775 they would find a new champion in the form of Henry Grattan.

BEER WAS BREWED in large quantities by the Irish

Henry Grattan and the Volunteers

With the outbreak of the American Revolution, the Irish seized the opportunity for greater freedom and independence from England.

Following the success of the Patriots in the Irish Parliament in the 1750s, a series of strong and uncompromising British viceroys stripped the Patriots of their power. Then, in 1776, the American colonies revolted against British rule.

THE DECLARATION of Independence, signed in 1776, saw the American colonies break free from the British Empire

HENRY GRATTAN (1746–1820)
the Patriot lawyer, was leader of the Irish Parliament

Politically, as well as geographically, Ireland sat between Britain and the American colonies, and the Revolution had a profound impact on the Irish. All of the British troops that had been stationed in Ireland were either withdrawn or sent to America, and the treasury was stripped bare in order to fund the war.

In response to being left undefended, the Irish Parliament, now led by the Patriot lawyer, Henry Grattan, gained the right to raise a Protestant militia force in 1778. By 1779, more than 40,000 Volunteers had signed up and even many Catholics, who were forbidden by the Penal Laws from bearing arms, supported the movement. With no specific enemy to fight, the Volunteers quickly became a force for political change. As the Irish MP, Walter Hussey Burgh, stated: 'England has sown her laws like dragon's teeth and they have sprung up in armed men'.

This unexpected display of Irish political unity and the problems of the continued American war, forced the British Parliament on to its back foot, and the Irish

GILLRAY'S 1798
cartoon of Grattan

Parliament pressed its advantage. Led by the stirring speeches of Grattan, the Irish called upon England to repeal its unfair trade laws. Backed into a corner, England complied. Celebrations were held across Ireland, but the Patriot leaders knew that the victory represented only the beginning. Because of Poynings' Law and the 1720 Declaratory Act, the British Parliament still had the right to enact or overturn any Irish legislation and could reinstate any of the trade laws at any time. Ireland needed full parliamentary independence.

By the time the Irish Parliament opened in 1782, the political landscape of Britain had changed. The British had lost the war in America and the defeat had swept the Tory government from office. The time to strike had come. On 16 April 1782, Henry Grattan arose and set Parliament alight with a cry for freedom: 'For acknowledging American liberty, England has the plea of necessity; for acknowledging the liberties of Ireland she has the plea of justice.' So powerful was Grattan's cry, that no one dared cast

MEETING AT DUNGANNON

On 25 February 1782, Volunteer leaders met at Dungannon and formed a declaration demanding legislative independence from the Irish Parliament. Despite this, the Irish remained loyal to the King, stating: 'We know our duty to our Sovereign, and we are loyal. We know our duty to ourselves, and are resolved to be Free'.

a dissenting vote. England, unable and unwilling to face another revolution, capitulated.

The victory for legislative independence ushered in a new era of Irish politics, and the next twenty years is often referred to as 'Grattan's Parliament' in honour of the achievement. Henry Grattan, meanwhile, turned his attention to a new problem – the continued suppression of Irish Catholics that festered beneath the surface of a reenergised Ireland.

IRISH PARLIAMENT was referred to as Grattan's Parliament

The Secret Societies: From the Whiteboys to the Orange Order

Amidst growing Irish Nationalism in the eighteenth century, a number of secret, violent organisations grew amongst the population.

To an outsider, Ireland in the second half of the eighteenth century was a blossoming country. A new wave of political action eventually led to legislative independence, while increased trade revenue and the booming economy built upon new industries brought revenue and jobs. However, to many of the Irish, the situation appeared very different. A huge spike in the population caused increased competition for farming land and soaring rent prices. The cities, especially Dublin, that served as centres for the new industries became overcrowded, causing slums to appear. Meanwhile, the underlying tension between the

ORANGE ORDER FLAG
features the English cross and the purple Williamite star

different religious groups continued to simmer unchecked. In the north, the Irish Catholics competed for land with the Scottish-descended Presbyterians, while the English Protestant minority continued to own most of the land and wield complete political power. Inevitably, cracks began to form.

In 1759, Britain removed previous restrictions against Irish cattle, causing a resurgent cattle market. In support, new legislation in Ireland closed off significant areas of common land for grazing, at the expense of many Irish Catholics who farmed and lived on the land.

IRISH PARLIAMENT
passed new legislation which angered Irish Catholics

Without any legal or political recourse against the British, the threatened Irish responded in the only way they could. Like the woodkerns before them, they formed into secret bands of nighttime marauders who destroyed enclosures, maimed livestock and assaulted the local cattlemen. The populace called these new groups 'Whiteboys', because of the white smocks they wore over their clothes.

Within a few years, societies had been formed by the Ulster Presbyterians, most notably the Hearts of Oak and the Hearts of Steel. Protesting against numerous injustices, they launched their own reign of terror against the English landlords. Considering that Irish Catholics and Presbyterians had little protection under the law, these secret societies took root and flowered, especially in Ulster. By the late eighteenth century, these two groups were competing for the same limited resources in the north, and both turned to their own secret societies to fight for their cause. The Presbyterians were represented by the Peep O' Day Boys, who attacked their enemies at dawn. The Catholics formed the Defenders, who proved significantly more offensive than defensive. Both sides used terrorism in an attempt to

MANY IRISH
Catholics were farmers, living off the land

drive the others out, and the violence quickly escalated.

In September 1795, the struggle between the Peep O' Day Boys and the Defenders reached a crescendo at a crossroads known as the Diamond. There, a group of Peep O' Day Boys, better armed and on their home ground, poured a hail of musket fire into an attacking group of Defenders. When the smoke cleared, dozens of Defender bodies littered the ground.

THE PEEP O'DAY BOYS
later became the
Orange Order

The Peep O' Day Boys marched off in celebration and later that day they reformed their society into the Orange Order, which would play an important part in Northern Irish politics for years to come.

The violence of the eighteenth century secret societies left a terrible legacy, especially in Northern Ireland, which still suffers from the crimes of these warring groups.

Wolfe Tone and the United Irishmen

Inspired by the French Revolution, Wolfe Tone and the United Irishmen pressed for the equality of all Irishmen, regardless of religious affiliation.

WOLFE TONE (1763–1798) helped form The Society of United Irishmen

THE FRENCH Revolution inspired Wolfe Tone and others in Ireland (facing page)

In 1791, the young Dublin-born lawyer Theobald Wolfe Tone released a pamphlet entitled *An Argument on Behalf of the Catholics of Ireland*, in which he argued that Catholics and Protestants should come together in a political union. For many who had been raised during the Protestant Ascendancy, Wolfe Tone's ideas were preposterous. But there were others, such as the famous politician Henry Grattan, who believed in the message and, later that year, the Society of United Irishmen was formed.

The next year proved to be a momentous one in European history. It was the year that the Reign of Terror began in France, plunging all of Europe into decades of brutal warfare. The government in England

THE SOCIETY OF UNITED IRISHMEN

In 1791, a group of Irish Volunteers from Belfast invited Wolfe Tone to help found a new organisation inspired by the French Revolution and devoted to the cause of equality. Christened 'The Society of United Irishmen,' they determined to reform the Parliament of Ireland, resolving that 'no reform is practicable, efficacious, or just, which shall not include Irishmen of every religious persuasion'. Although the founding members of the group were all Protestants, their membership grew to include numerous Catholics. The Society spread out of Dublin and, later in the year, it started its own newspaper, the Northern Star, which quickly became the most read newspaper in Ireland. The Society also organised the Belfast Harp Festival to promote an important piece of Irish Catholic culture. Yet, despite these efforts, the Society could do little to sway the majority of Protestants who sat in the Irish Parliament.

began to worry about the oppressed masses that made up the majority in Ireland. In 1793, the Catholic Committee from Ireland, including Henry Grattan and Wolfe Tone, travelled to England and met with King George III and Prime Minister William Pitt the Younger. The meeting proved a tremendous success, and the Committee returned to Ireland with assurances of help from the King and Prime Minister. Later that year, thanks to wholesale bribery, the Irish Parliament voted to repeal nearly all of the Penal Laws. Catholics could once again own land and even vote in parliamentary elections. Only the prohibition against serving in Parliament and other top government postings remained. The Irish Catholics celebrated and even cast a special medal for Wolfe Tone, but the United Irishmen saw their job as only half done.

GEORGE III (1738–1820) had a successful meeting with Wolfe Tone

When Henry Grattan's bill proposing full Catholic emancipation met with defeat, many in the United Irishmen thought to continue the political debate by other means. In 1795, Wolfe Tone was arrested for meeting with a French spy and only managed to save his life by going into exile in America. He soon left America for France, where he convinced the French government that Ireland stood on the brink of rebellion. The French organised a vast expedition of 45,000 soldiers to sail to Ireland to fan the fires of revolution, but the attempt ended in farce. Forced by the strength of the Royal Navy to sail during the winter, the expedition became separated in a storm and lost its commanding officer. Although most of the fleet did arrive in Ireland, the horrendous weather prevented a landing, and the expedition was abandoned.

With the failure of the French invasion, the British moved quickly in Ireland, rounding up the leaders of the United Irishmen. But it was too late. In May 1798, Ireland exploded into open warfare.

FRENCH SHIPS
were unable to land in Ireland, due to bad weather

General Lake and the Wexford War

In 1798, an isolated rebellion quickly exploded into the ugliest and bloodiest revolt in the history of the Anglo-Irish relationship.

**GENERAL LAKE
(1744–1808)**
had almost full
authority in Ulster

With the failure of the French invasion in 1796 and the ongoing violence between the Defenders and the Orangemen in Ulster, the government passed the Insurrection Act, which gave nearly full authority in Ulster to the local British military commander, General Gerard Lake. Using a network of informants, Lake rounded up most of the leaders of the United Irishmen, whilst loosing the locally recruited Yeomanry on the countryside in search of weapons.

In response to Yeoman brutality, the ranks of the United Irishmen and their new militant allies, the Defenders, swelled into tens of thousands. The last of the United Irishmen leaders still at large, Lord Edward Fitzgerald, declared that they would rise up on 23 May

1798. However, on 19 May, the authorities captured
Lord Edward in Dublin in a bloody scene similar to an
Old West gunfight. Leaderless, the rising went ahead.
Within two days, thousands of Irishmen took up arms,
mainly pikes and farm implements, and fought over
a dozen battles in County Kildare. In most places, the
British forces recovered from their initial surprise and
fought back, easily defeating the disorganised and
poorly armed Irish. But the worst was yet to come.

YEOMAN BRUTALITY

Although General Lake succeeded in disarming most of
the populace, the brutal methods of the mostly untrained
Yeomanry did more to spark rebellion than to suppress it.
Their tortures included half-hanging, flogging and pitchcapping
– where hot pitch (or tar) mixed with gunpowder was poured
on a suspect's head and set on fire. When the commander
of all British Forces in Ireland, General Sir Ralph Abercromby,
reported to the British government that its soldiers were out
of control, he was forced out of office and replaced with Lake.

Pitchcapping

The initial flame of rebellion soon died down, but a series of bloody reprisals by the British forces stoked the fears of many Irish, both Catholic and Protestant alike. It was rumoured that the British were on a campaign of genocide. The people of Counties Wicklow and Wexford then rose up in rebellion under the leadership of Father John Murphy, a Catholic Priest. The rebels seized the city of Wexford and declared the Irish Republic. However, this short-lived republic is most notable for the atrocities it committed against loyalists, including 100 prisoners who were stabbed to death with pikes.

For a time, the entire eastern half of Ireland seemed to be ablaze, as loyalist fought rebel. But, with no central leadership, the United Irishmen and Defenders could not compete with the increasingly well organised British response.

IRISH FREEDOM
fighter depicted by a statue in Wexford

Slowly the British forces drew together, driving the rebels before them, until they stood before Vinegar Hill, on the outskirts of Wexford. Nearly 20,000 Irish rebels, armed with pikes, stood against 10,000 British soldiers, backed by numerous cannons. The result was a mass slaughter. The British routed the Irish from the hill, chasing them through the streets of Wexford, granting no quarter or mercy, even burning down the hospital with the wounded still inside.

VINEGAR HILL
near Wexford was the scene of a bloody slaughter

After his victory at Wexford, Lake was recalled to Britain and replaced with the more restrained Lord Cornwallis. With most of the fighting over, Cornwallis granted an amnesty, ending the rebellion.

It is estimated that more than 30,000 Irish died in the rebellions; most were non-combatants. In a final, ironic twist, just as the rebellion ended, Wolfe Tone and the French once again set sail for Ireland. It was too little and far too late.

The Act of Union

Following the 1798 rebellions, the British Prime Minister, William Pitt, battled against the Irish Parliament to create a union of the two nations.

For the British Government, the timing of the Irish rebellions of 1798 could not have been worse. Despite the failure of the French invasions of Ireland, the forces of revolutionary France proved unstoppable on the continent, repeatedly defeating Britain and her allies. The danger of an unstable Ireland, at a time when its total population was nearly half that of all of Great Britain, left Prime Minister William Pitt considering a radical solution. He sent Lord Cornwallis to restore order and appointed Robert Stewart (Lord Castlereagh) as Chief Secretary, instructing both men to begin work on a proposed Act of Union, that would merge the parliaments of Britain and Ireland.

WILLIAM PITT (1759–1806) addressing the House of Commons at Westminster

After the violence of the last year, many in Ireland were open to the idea of change. Cornwallis and Castlereagh first approached the leaders of the Catholic Church in Ireland. They promised state support for the church and, with William Pitt's blessing, they hinted that the Act of Union would lead to full emancipation of Ireland's Catholics. Soon, most Irish Catholics, at least those who paid any attention to politics, supported the Union. However, the majority of the Catholic-free Irish Parliament did not.

IRISH CATHOLICS were promised full emancipation after the Act of Union

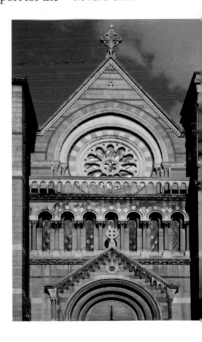

When Parliament reconvened in January 1799, the Act of Union was the only topic. The debate lasted through the night, with no less than 80 MPs voicing their opinion. When a vote finally came, the Union won by a single vote; but in such an unstable environment this paltry margin was not enough for the Parliament to vote its own demise.

BRIBERY AND CORRUPTION

As a pamphlet war for and against the Union raged, Cornwallis and Castlereagh turned to bribery and inducements to curry votes, offering peerages, pensions and cash. Although this blatant vote buying was not illegal, Lord Cornwallis found it extremely distasteful, commenting: 'I despise and hate myself every hour engaging in such dirty work.' Still, success followed the moves and slowly Parliament began to shift in their favour.

On 15 January 1800, Lord Castlereagh again brought the Act of Union before the Parliament, and the war of words began anew. Henry Grattan led the opposition, having come out of retirement to fight against the act. Despite an illness which confined him to his chair, he spoke for two hours in an attempt to preserve the independence he had fought so hard to gain. So vehemently did he rail against the act that it eventually led him into a pistol duel with the Irish Chancellor of the Exchequer. It was

THE UNION JACK represents all the countries of the United Kingdom

all to no avail. Reasoned argument could not compete with bribery, and the Act of Union was passed by sixty votes.

One year later, the Irish Parliament disbanded, while 100 Irish representatives took up seats in the House of Commons in Westminster, joined by 32 new members of the House of Lords. For the time the two countries kept their own treasuries, but together they formed one nation – The United Kingdom of Great Britain and Ireland.

THE ACT OF UNION made Great Britain and Ireland into one country

With the success of the Act of Union, William Pitt turned his attention to Catholic emancipation, but it soon became clear that neither the Parliament nor the King would ever agree to such an idea. The aged King George III, suffering from mental deterioration, claimed that such a move would violate his oath to uphold the Church of England (now merged with that of Ireland). Unwilling to start a fight that could damage the fragile Union, William Pitt did the only thing left open to him; he resigned, as did Lord Cornwallis and Lord Castlereagh.

Robert Emmet

Robert Emmet's rebellion played out like a black comedy, and it is only the dignity of his death that has assured his place as an Irish folk hero.

ROBERT EMMET (1778–1803)
kept the revolutionary spirit alive in Ireland

Despite the political turmoil created by the Act of Union in 1800, it brought little immediate change to Ireland. The Protestants remained firmly on top, safe in their positions of power, while deep social unrest continued to cause outbreaks of violence and lawlessness. Even with the ongoing war against France, nearly 25,000 British soldiers remained on permanent station in Ireland. The United Irishmen and the Defenders may have been beaten in 1798, but the embers of both organisations

THE SEEDS OF REVOLUTION

Expelled from Trinity College in 1798 for his connections to the United Irishmen, Robert Emmet helped hold the organisation together in the wake of the disastrous rebellions.

In 1799, he travelled to France to join the growing United Irishman lobby. He returned in 1802, with a pocket full of French promises and a head full of revolutionary ideas.

still burned hot and soon they found new leadership in the young, adventurous Robert Emmet.

Using money from his inheritance, Emmet established a number of secret weapons factories in the heart of Dublin. Blessed with a creative mind, Emmet designed new varieties of explosives, including rockets and grenades that his factories churned out alongside the now ubiquitous pike. Emmet also met with other revolutionary groups in and around Dublin and devised a plan to seize Dublin castle as the opening phase of a general revolt.

On 23 May the revolution leaders met with Emmet and attempted to talk him out of the plan, but Emmet would not be dissuaded. He called his men to gather at a local tavern, while he secured the coaches that would drive them all to Dublin Castle. Of the 2,000 men Emmet expected, only about 80 showed up, and most of these proceeded to get drunk in the tavern. Then Emmet learned of a mix-up with the fuses for the rockets and grenades that rendered the weapons useless. To top

DUBLIN CASTLE was the scene of Emmet's failed plot

it all off, when the coaches finally arrived, the coach drivers got spooked and drove off into the night. His revolution already in shambles, Robert Emmet drew his sword and led his drunken, pike-armed mob through the street calling out, 'Now is your time for liberty'. Before the group had marched far, most of Emmet's men had drifted away. Dejected and defeated, Robert Emmet gave up and went home, only to be berated by his housekeeper for abandoning his men.

Unfortunately, the story of the revolt did not end there. A mob containing some of Emmet's men continued to rampage through the Dublin streets until they encountered Lord Kilwarden, the chief justice of the King's Bench. The drunken mob pulled the popular justice from his coach and stabbed both him and his son to death.

A month after the failed rebellion, the authorities found and arrested Robert Emmet. He put up no defence at his trial. On the day of his execution, Emmet stood on the docks and supposedly said, 'When my

LORD KILWARDEN was pulled from his coach and assassinated by a drunken mob

country takes her place among the nations of the earth, then, and only then, let my epitaph be written.' Robert Emmet was buried in an unmarked grave.

The history of Ireland is strewn with tragic heroes like Robert Emmet, whose ideals and poetry far outweighed their common sense or tactical ability. From Silken Thomas to Wolfe Tone and on to the leaders of the Easter Rising, these men are all remembered as folk heroes who kept the revolutionary spirit alive, until one day Ireland could be free.

Daniel O'Connell, Liberator of the Nation

Daniel O'Connell became a champion of Catholic Emancipation in Ireland and, eventually, the first Irish Catholic to sit in the British Parliament.

DANIEL O'CONNELL (1775–1847) became a champion of Catholic Emancipation

In 1804, Ireland's greatest politician, Henry Grattan, put aside his bitterness and disgust at the Act of Union, and won a seat in the new united Parliament in Westminster. Unable to find any support for a repeal of the Union, Grattan set his energy to his other great aim, Catholic Emancipation. Even though the Catholic Relief Act of 1793 had given the vote to anyone in Ireland who owned the minimal 40 shillings' worth of property, Catholics were still not allowed in Parliament and thus could not represent themselves. Year after year, Henry Grattan gathered support for the movement, watching as the margin of defeat for his emancipation bills shrank every time. In 1819, his bill lost by a mere two votes. In 1820, worn out by a life devoted to his country, Henry Grattan died. Later that year, his supporters put forward a new emancipation bill that passed the House of Commons. The House of Lords rejected it.

Although many in the Protestant Ascendancy rejoiced, most of Ireland felt betrayed. With Henry Grattan dead, they searched for another hero to lead

THE HOUSE OF LORDS
had the power of veto over legislation

their cause. They found him in a Catholic lawyer named Daniel O'Connell. Educated in law in France and England, O'Connell returned to Ireland in 1797, just as the fires of rebellion were spreading across the country. Witnessing these horrors, O'Connell decided, 'Liberty is not worth the shedding of a single drop of blood.' For years, O'Connell built his reputation as a Dublin lawyer, while working to unify his fellow Catholic countrymen. Then, in 1824, he struck upon a new formula. Having helped found a new political organisation, The Catholic Association, the year before, O'Connell reduced the membership fee to a penny a month. Membership exploded. The Catholic Church got involved, helping to collect the dues, which soon became known as 'Catholic Rent'. £20,000 was raised in the first year. Terrified of this new movement, the British government outlawed the Catholic Association in 1825. Four months later, Daniel O'Connell founded 'The New Catholic Association', listing among its principles full compliance with the laws of Britain.

Aided by this new unity, Catholics in Waterford, led by Thomas Wyse and Father John Sheehan, recruited a Protestant to run as an 'emancipation' candidate in the Parliamentary election against the local landlord. Although all forty-shilling freeholders could vote, the ballot was not secret and those voting against the will of their landlord risked retribution. When O'Connell later added the weight of the Catholic Association to the cause, the emancipation candidate won by a landslide. Meanwhile, the Catholic Association supported any Catholic Irish who suffered reprisals from the landlord.

Two years later, and with two emancipation candidates in Parliament, O'Connell discovered a legal loophole. The last of the Penal Laws didn't actually prevent a Catholic from being elected to Parliament; it just required an oath that no true Catholic could ever give. So, when a by-election was forced in County Clare in 1828, O'Connell stood for election. More than 30,000 Catholic Association supporters descended on a town that had but 3,000 voters. On election day, O'Connell captured over 2,000 votes and set off for Westminster. When O'Connell arrived at Parliament, he refused to take the oath.

The British government saw that they were beaten. In 1829, the Emancipation bill became law. O'Connell, now given the title 'Liberator of the Nation', took his seat in Parliament, while the Catholic Association disbanded.

However, in a calculated epilogue, the British government raised the minimum holding for Irish voters from forty shillings to ten pounds. Overnight, over 90 per cent of the Irish electorate lost their vote.

DANIEL O'CONNELL
depicted in a
statue in Dublin

Young Ireland and the Repeal Movement

After the success of his Emancipation Movement, O'Connell turned his energy to the repeal of the Union and gained new allies in Young Ireland.

BELFAST UNDERWENT a huge industrial boom

For several years after his election to Parliament, Daniel O'Connell became an important figure in the political machinations of Westminster. Leading a group of 40 or so Irish MPs, he pushed for the repeal of the Act of Union and a return to the days of Grattan's Parliament, when Ireland and Britain had been separate nations under the rule of the same monarch. But most British politicians saw little to be gained by repeal, and even in Ireland opinion remained divided, especially in the north, where Protestants tended to support the Union. The years since the Act of Union had proved beneficial in the north, with a decrease in sectarian violence

YOUNG IRELAND

Young Ireland, led by Thomas Davis, Charles Gavan Duffy and John Blake Dillon, was a mixed Catholic and Protestant group, formed to promote Irish nationalism.

(caused by religious prejudice) and an industrial boom, which saw the population of Belfast triple. In the south, however, the higher number of Catholics and the more agrarian economy tended to set people against the Union.

In 1838, O'Connell decided to take his battle away from Parliament and back to the people of Ireland. He began his campaign in the divided province of Ulster, but his presence caused so much civil unrest that he quickly returned to the south. There he set up a new

THOMAS DAVIS (1814-1845) was one of the leaders of Young Ireland

THE NATION

To support their cause, Young Ireland launched *The Nation*. It soon became the most-read newspaper in Ireland, selling 250,000 copies each week.

organisation, the Repeal Association, modelled on the Catholic Association. The penny a month membership was now called 'Repeal Rent', and with the help of the Catholic Church, money flowed in.

Aided by Young Ireland and the Catholic Church, O'Connell held 'Monster Meetings' which, although peaceful, were designed to scare the government in Britain. The plan worked all too well.

O'Connell decided to hold a 'Monster Meeting' at Clontarf, near Dublin, where Brian Bóru had won his great victory over the Vikings. Then, on the day before the meeting, the government outlawed the gathering. Although it is unlikely that Britain could have stopped

BRIAN BÓRÚ
whose victory at Clontarf was echoed in the 'Monster Meetings'

MONSTER MEETINGS

With the help of The Nation, in 1843 Daniel O'Connell organised a series of huge demonstrations all over the south of Ireland. Dubbed, 'Monster Meetings,' by the Times, these gatherings attracted hundreds of thousands of people. The largest took place on the hill of Tara, ancient seat of the Irish kings. Nearly three quarters of a million Irish attended to hear O'Connell speak.

the hundreds of thousands of people planning to attend, O'Connell stayed true to his notions of non-violence. With the help of Young Ireland, the meeting was called off.

Soon after, O'Connell was arrested for treason and sentenced to a year in prison but, on his arrival at Richmond prison, the warden let O'Connell stay in his house. The conviction was later overturned by the House of Lords and O'Connell was set free.

O'Connell now tempered his views and called for a separate Irish Parliament to decide on domestic issues, with Westminster controlling foreign affairs. This call for compromise lost O'Connell some support and opened a rift with Young Ireland. As it turned out, the break made little difference. In the next few years, a catastrophe overwhelmed Ireland and made most political movements superfluous: the Great Famine struck.

DANIEL O'CONNELL addressing a 'Monster Meeting'

The Great Famine

Perhaps the single most important event in modern Irish history, the potato famine led to the deaths of nearly a million people and the emigration of over a million more.

In 1843, the British Government established the Devon Commission to investigate and comment upon the effect of the ballooning Irish population on the Irish land system. Having seen the Irish population grow from five million in 1800 to over eight million by 1841, many in government

STARVING PEOPLE attacked a government potato store at the height of the famine

POTATO BLIGHT

In recent years, the potato blight has been identified as phytophthora infestans, an airborne fungus which originated in America. However, in 1846, the blight probably seemed more like an evil curse. Whole crops of potatoes just melted away into piles of infected, stinking goo.

worried that the small island could no longer fully support its inhabitants. In 1844, the Commission returned its findings, noting that huge segments of the population lived in abject poverty and stating that 'their only food is the potato'. In fact, by 1845 as many as three million Irish were wholly dependent on the potato for food. Then, in 1846, a new potato blight struck Ireland, and the crop began to fail.

In Britain, the Prime Minister, Robert Peel, responded quickly to the crisis. Quietly spending £1 million buying American corn, Peel sent the food to Ireland and distributed it to the hungry. For a while it appeared that the crisis might be averted, but then two events changed the history of Ireland.

In late 1846, the Whigs (the opposing party) drove Robert Peel from power, and in 1847 the potato blight returned to Ireland.

Unlike the 1846 blight, which mainly affected Ulster and the west coast

ROBERT PEEL (1788–1850) responded quickly to the crisis by sending food to Ireland

of Ireland, the blight of 1847 devastated the entire island. The Whig government, headed by Lord John Russell, instated a new work for food programme that proved to be an unwieldy, bureaucratic nightmare. Hunger killed the Irish by the thousands, and with the starvation came sickness and disease. And all the while, grain continued to be exported from Ireland to Britain. The government refused to stop the exports, fearing that it might upset the market.

HUNGER LED people to collect limpets and seaweed

IRISH MIGRATION

Irish migration had been occurring for over a century, but the Great Famine escalated the movement to previously unimagined levels. In the decade following 1845, over a million Irish left their homeland, most for the New World (America). The poor Irish crowded on to any ship that would take them, and unscrupulous ship captains took advantage. Thousands died in the ocean crossing, crammed aboard overloaded ships that became known as 'coffin ships'. More died while trying to clear customs, or attempting to walk from Canada to the United States. Still, hundreds of thousands made it through the horrors to establish new homes on these foreign shores, and created Irish enclaves that would play an important part in the future of Ireland.

Where the British government failed, others tried desperately to fight the crisis. The Society of Friends, or Quakers, set up food kitchens. American sympathisers sent food and money to Ireland. But it was not enough. The numbers of dead climbed into the hundreds of thousands, and the increasing desperation started a mass migration.

The year 1849 brought another ruined crop, only to be followed by a massive outbreak of cholera. By 1850, the population in Ireland had dropped to around six million. A quarter of the population had been wiped away; a million dead, a million more fled. When the blight failed to return in 1850, the Irish began to rebuild their island, but many did so with an even greater hatred for the British Government, which had seemingly abandoned them.

'COFFIN SHIPS' were overcrowded and many people died during the voyages

IRISH MIGRATION escalated as thousands boarded 'coffin ships' in search of a better life

The Irish Republican Brotherhood and the Fenians

The Irish Republican Brotherhood and their American allies, the Fenians, brought Ireland forcefully into the British consciousness.

THE FRENCH
Revolution taught
Stephens how to
stir up a revolt

When the 'Year of Revolutions' struck Europe in 1848, Ireland was realising the full horrors of the Great Famine. Despite their revolutionary history, the starving Irish managed only a small rising, organised by the leaders of Young Ireland. The revolt ended disappointingly, with a gun battle in a Dublin cabbage patch. Young Ireland was finished, but one of the battle's veterans, James Stephens, slipped quietly out of Ireland to take refuge in France. In the backrooms of Paris, Stephens learned the ways of revolution from the masters of the art.

On his return to Ireland in 1856, James Stephens began a 3,000 mile walk among Ireland's poor, looking for the embers of revolution. In 1858, he founded a new organisation, called the Irish Republican Brotherhood

(IRB), dedicated to the expulsion of the British and the foundation of an Irish Republic by any means available. While building the IRB, Stephens sought support from Irish expatriates in America, and eventually made contact with John O'Mahony.

O'Mahony had founded his own organisation in the United States, dedicated to Irish Republicanism. Named the Fenian Brotherhood, or Fenians, after a group of ancient Irish warriors, these revolutionaries quickly teamed up with the IRB to plot a joint revolution.

JAMES STEPHENS (1825–1901) founded the Irish Republican Brotherhood

The first step was increasing recruitment. In 1861, the IRB and the Fenians organised a large funeral parade for one of the participants of the 1848 revolt, who had died in America. The Fenians sent the body back to Ireland where Stephens and the IRB escorted it through the streets of Dublin. The funeral proved a massive success, and IRB membership shot up into the hundreds of thousands.

When the American Civil War broke out in 1861, rebellion was put on hold, but it provided an opportunity for many Fenians and other Irish volunteers to pick up valuable military experience. When the war ended in 1865, thousands of veteran Irish soldiers were ready to fight for Irish freedom. But, at that moment, Stephens faltered. Unable to organise a concerted strike, he gave Britain the opportunity it needed. Having infiltrated the IRB over the previous years, Britain quickly arrested many of the IRB leaders, including Stephens.

Although the IRB rescued Stephens from jail, the organisation had lost its cohesion. In May 1866, a group of impatient Fenians launched their own attack, from New York into Canada. They defeated a Canadian force at the Battle of Lime Ridge, but were later surrounded and broken up by a force from the United States. Having lost much of their Fenian support, the IRB launched their own disorganised revolution in March of 1867.

THE AMERICAN
Civil War gave many Fenians valuable military experience

THE MANCHESTER MARTYRS

In September 1867, three IRB members were hanged in Manchester for their part in murdering a policeman. Known as the 'Manchester Martyrs', the three spoke bravely of the suffering of Ireland as they stood upon the gallows, and newspapers across Britain published their final words.

Thousands rose up and marched on centres of authority in Ireland, but they lacked leadership and the revolt quickly sputtered out. In most cases, small groups of Irish constabulary dispersed the revolutionaries without recourse to violence.

Although ultimately unsuccessful, the revolts of the IRB and the Fenians raised British awareness of the plight of Ireland. The IRB would continue to play a role as Ireland's biggest secret revolutionary organisation, right up to the Easter Rising, but it was probably the awakening of the British consciousness to the case of Ireland that remains their most important legacy.

William Gladstone

In his four stints as Prime Minister, William Gladstone made justice for Ireland and the Irish people his foremost priority.

One day in December of 1868, the leader of the British Liberal Party, William Ewart Gladstone, picked up his axe and went outside to chop wood. As he worked, a messenger arrived and declared that Queen Victoria requested him to form a government, as his party had won the election. Gladstone lowered his axe and said: 'My mission is to pacify Ireland.'

WILLIAM GLADSTONE (1809–1898)
made justice for Ireland his priority

THE EARLY YEARS

Born in Liverpool in 1809, Gladstone received his education from Eton and Oxford. Originally, his deep religious faith drew him to the church, but eventually he decided that he could make a more significant contribution in politics. In his early political years, Gladstone showed little sympathy for Ireland, even aiding the movement that removed Prime Minister Robert Peel during the Great Famine.

Impressed by the courage and determination of the Fenians (as the British often called members of the IRB) and especially the 'Manchester Martyrs', Gladstone took a careful examination of the Irish question and saw the many injustices alive in the country.

Despite his own religious convictions, Gladstone first focused his attention on the dissolution of the Church of Ireland. In a country of over six million people, only around 700,000 Irish belonged to the so-called 'national' church. By making his fellow countrymen aware of this discrepancy, Gladstone pushed through a bill that brought an end to the national church in Ireland. The church kept the buildings it used for worship, but the rest of the land passed to the government.

Gladstone put forward the revolutionary idea that the land be sold to the tenants who lived and worked there. Given financial assistance from the government, thousands of Irish bought property for the first time. The bill also ended the hated tithe payment and all government obligations to the Catholic and

THE DISSOLUTION of the Church of Ireland became the focus of Gladstone's attention

Presbyterian Churches. The government completely removed itself from the business of religion in Ireland.

Gladstone then turned his efforts to Ireland's biggest problem; the ongoing land disputes. For years, the greedy and often unscrupulous landlords had milked the Irish for every penny, in a system that discouraged land improvement and kept the Irish living in fear of eviction. In 1870, Gladstone put forward a bill that would give protection from unfair evictions to tenants and ensure that they received the benefits of any improvements they made on the land they worked. Although the bill passed through Commons, the House of Lords completely reworked it. The Land Act of 1870 became a mostly toothless law, which provoked outrage in much of Ireland and helped to contribute to the violence and unlawfulness known as the Land War.

Soon after this failure, Gladstone fell out of power and sat on the sidelines as the next administration

THE LAND WAR
was a result of Irish outrage following the passing of the Land Act in 1870

mostly ignored Ireland. In 1880, the Liberals won the election, and Gladstone returned to the post of Prime Minister. Immediately, he tried to set things right in Ireland. His new Land Act of 1881 provided yet more protection for Irish renters, but it was not enough. In order to end the violence of the Land War, Gladstone reluctantly signed the Coercion Acts, which gave far-reaching powers to arrest and hold dissidents. Although the moves helped end the Land War, they contrived to increase discontent in many areas. Before he could return to the problem, Gladstone resigned in 1885 over the Khartoum affair, which saw the death of the popular General Gordon.

But Gladstone was not finished. Despite his advanced age and his unpopularity with Queen Victoria, who described him as a 'half-crazy and in many ways ridiculous old man', Gladstone would return twice more as Prime Minster. Those two terms would be notable for his relationship to Charles Parnell and the great battle for Home Rule.

QUEEN VICTORIA (1819–1901) regarded Gladstone as 'a ridiculous old man'

CHARLES PARNELL
depicted in a
statue in Dublin

Charles Stewart Parnell

One of Ireland's greatest politicians, Charles Parnell took the fight for the rights of Ireland into the heart of Westminster.

After the failure of the Fenian cause in the 1860s, the oppressed Irish once again turned to politics to try to right the wrongs of the past. In 1870, a former Trinity College professor, Isaac Butt, founded the Home Rule Association and won a seat in Parliament, as the head of the new Home Rule Party. Like Daniel O'Connell, the Home Rulers wanted a return to the days of

OBSTRUCTION

The policy of 'obstruction' was invented by a former butcher from Belfast, named Joseph Biggar, in order to make Irish voices heard in Westminster. Biggar tied up Parliament for hours by speaking at length on irrelevant topics and endlessly proposing additions to legislation. Obstruction became even more effective when practised by a young, energetic, Irish politician named Charles Stewart Parnell.

Grattan's Parliament, when Ireland and Britain stood independently under the same monarch. They were soon to find a new champion, in the form of Charles Stewart Parnell.

An Irish Protestant educated at Cambridge, Parnell quickly rose through the ranks of the Home Rule Party by becoming the champion of the Irish common man. In the late 1870s, several years of bad weather destroyed much of Ireland's agriculture and sent thousands of Irish farmers into a cycle of debt that they could not escape. In an effort to defend their homes, they formed the Land League, with Charles Parnell as their president. Although Parnell had secretly secured the support of the IRB, he preached a non-violent solution to the problem. He advocated a policy of shunning, which meant that people should refuse to deal with any landlord who unfairly evicted their tenants, or any Irish who took up the rent of the newly available land. The movement became known as the Land War and it continuously teetered on the brink of lawlessness. In 1879, the Land League achieved its greatest success when their move to

CHARLES PARNELL (1846–1891) was one of Ireland's greatest politicians

POLITICAL CARTOON
depicting Charles
Parnell as a
vampire bat

shun the British Captain Boycott gained international press and coined the term 'boycotting'.

In 1881, Prime Minister Gladstone tried to end the Land War by passing a new Land Act, but the Land League refused to accept it. As tension grew, the chief secretary in Ireland had Parnell arrested. Parnell instantly became an Irish hero and could have launched a massive uprising but, to his credit, he sought a peaceful solution. Six months after his arrest, Parnell and Gladstone reached an accord with the Kilmainham Treaty. Parnell left prison in support of the new Land Act.

In 1882, Ireland was rocked by a new crisis: the Irish Chief Secretary and his Under-Secretary were murdered in Phoenix Park by an off-shoot of the IRB. Parnell, now the most powerful man in Ireland, condemned the murders and used the incident to break from all violent extremist groups in Ireland.

Parnell now turned his attention back to Home Rule, and by 1885 his party had secured 85 seats in Parliament. The number allowed the Home Rulers to oust the Conservatives in favour of Gladstone's Liberal party. Gladstone and Parnell campaigned for Irish Home Rule, but the issue proved too great for them to handle. Gladstone's Liberal party began to come apart over the issue, while Parnell's private life fell to pieces.

When the vote for Home Rule came, many Liberals voted against their leader. Home Rule was defeated. Two years later, a worn-out Parnell died, aged 45.

PARNELL'S RESIGNATION

Unknown to most, Parnell had carried on an affair with Katherine ('Kitty') O'Shea, the wife of a British Captain, since 1880. Slowly, rumours began to circulate and, in 1889, Captain O'Shea filed for a divorce. In the height of Victorian Britain, a divorce was almost unheard of, and it became a national news event. Catholic Bishops withdrew their support from Parnell and many within the Liberal party also rebelled. Gladstone had no choice but to ask Parnell to resign.

Katherine O'Shea

The Gaelic League and the Gaelic Athletic Association

Growing out of Ireland's search for a national identity, the Gaelic League and the Gaelic Athletic Association worked to revive the ancient Irish culture. Both organisations have lasted over a century and continue to play an important part in Irish life and politics.

MICHAEL CUSACK (1847–1906) founded the Gaelic Athletic Association

When Young Ireland formed in 1842, it included amongst its goals the renewal of the Irish language and culture. For nearly 500 years, the English had chipped away at the Irish, suppressing their education and obscuring their rich cultural past. When the years of famine and revolution wiped away Young Ireland, it nearly took Irish culture with it. The poor Irish, who carried the legacy of the ancient past, suffered the brunt of the Great Famine.

By 1851, less than a quarter of the population spoke Irish. Forty years later, the number had dropped below 15 per cent. But, as a new nationalism swept through Ireland toward the end of the nineteenth century, the Irish looked to their past to help define their country. In those dying days, the Irish grabbed hold of their remaining culture and fought to bring it back from the point of extinction.

THE LEGEND
of Setanta is an early reference to the sport of hurling

THE FOUNDING OF THE GAA

The Gaelic Athletic Association (GAA) was founded by Michael Cusack in 1884. Cusack had grown up as a fan of rugby and cricket, but he became disenchanted with the social exclusiveness and gambling associated with these sports. In an effort to escape those pitfalls and to improve the national morale, he created the GAA to promote sport among the Irish of all classes. The organisation originally focused on athletics, but this soon gave way to the ancient Gaelic games of Gaelic football and hurling.

**EOIN MACNEILL
(1867–1945)**
helped to found
the Gaelic League

The Gaelic Athletic Association was a great success. With the growing prosperity of the Victorian era, spectator sports experienced a tremendous growth in popularity, and in Ireland this combined with the growing nationalism, partly inspired by the GAA. Within a few years, the IRB had completely usurped power in the GAA, ousted Cusack and made the organisation even more obviously nationalistic. Players and fans were not allowed to participate in, or even watch, any 'foreign' sports. By the early 1900s, the most important GAA matches attracted over 20,000 spectators.

As the GAA brought the ancient Irish games back to public awareness, others worked to do the same for the Irish language. In 1893, a group of academics, that included Eoin MacNeill, founded the Gaelic League to support Irish, as both a spoken language and a language for literature. The Gaelic League ran classes in Irish, held Irish-speaking social gatherings and sponsored the publication of contemporary poetry and prose in Irish. Soon it also took on a political role; fighting against any legislation that it believed would have a detrimental effect on the language, and proposing legislation to help in its revival.

GAELIC FOOTBALL is a popular sport in Ireland today

Although the Gaelic League and the GAA became entangled in violent nationalistic struggles, waged by various organisations, both managed to survive and even prosper. Today, the GAA has over 2,500 clubs in Ireland and interest in Gaelic football and hurling is as strong as ever. It has even dropped most of its nationalist rules, including the ban on watching and playing foreign games. Meanwhile, the Gaelic League, or *Connradh na Gaeilge* in Gaelic, carries on its quest to reinstate Irish as the common language of Ireland. With over 200 branches, it continues to hold classes, support literature and argue for legislation in support of the ancient tongue.

William Butler Yeats

Commonly regarded as Ireland's greatest poet, Yeats combined a brilliant literary career with a turbulent personal life.

**W. B. YEATS
(1865–1939)**
is widely regarded as
Ireland's greatest poet

William Butler Yeats was born in Dublin on 13 June 1865, to an Anglo-Irish family. His father, who had abandoned a career in law in favour of painting, moved the family back and forth between Dublin and London in pursuit of his dreams. Although young William grew up as a child of two countries, he soon fell in love with the stories of the mythical Irish past. William could not read Irish but, even so, the tales and names that made it into English fired his imagination and greatly influenced a growing talent for poetry. In 1885, *The Dublin University Review* became the first publisher of Yeats's poetry.

Four years later, Yeats came to national attention with the publication of his book, *The Wanderings of Oisin and Other Poems*.

'THE SONG OF THE HAPPY SHEPHERD'

An excerpt from Yeats's poem 'The Song of the Happy Shepherd'

Where are now the warring kings?
An idle word is now their glory,
By the stammering schoolboy said,
Reading some entangled story:
The kings of the old time are dead;...

Just as Yeats's professional life began to blossom, his personal life took a dark turn. In 1889, Yeats met Maud Gonne, a young heiress with an intense belief in Irish Nationalism. Yeats fell completely in love with Gonne and, two years later, he proposed. Gonne turned him down. Although Yeats's poetry during this period contained a growing sense of Irish Nationalism, it was not enough for Gonne. She turned down his proposals on three more occasions, before marrying John MacBride (who would later be executed for his part in the Easter Rising).

MAUD GONNE (1866–1953) turned down a number of marriage proposals from Yeats

THE IRISH LITERARY THEATRE

In 1896, still deep in his infatuation for Maud Gonne, Yeats became friends with Lady Gregory, a nationalist widow, who encouraged Yeats to pursue his growing interest in writing drama. In 1899, Yeats, Gregory and others founded the Irish Literary Theatre to perform plays written in Irish or with a strong Irish theme. The theatre became one of the cornerstones of the Irish Literary Revival and played a strong role in the continued growth of Irish Nationalism. This theatre still exists in Dublin under the more common name of the Abbey Theatre.

W. B. YEATS
photographed in 1911

As the nineteenth century passed into the twentieth, an older, more mature Yeats developed a new poetic style; abandoning the earlier lyrical mysticism for more direct imagery. But the change in style may not have represented a change of heart. In 1916, after the execution of John MacBride, Yeats proposed once again to Maude Gonne. When she turned him down, he proposed to her daughter, who also rejected him. A few weeks later, he proposed to Georgie Hyde-Lees, a woman 25 years his junior. She accepted, and the couple had a long marriage that produced two children, despite Yeats's constant infidelity.

In December of 1923, Yeats received the Nobel Prize in Literature, a first for an Irishman. He continued to write poetry, and many argue that his best works were produced after receiving the award. Also around this time, Yeats served two terms in the Irish Senate, notably leading the argument for the legalisation of divorce.

THE IRISH LANDSCAPE provided inspiration for Yeats's poetry

Yeats died on 28 January 1939, aged 73. At the time of his death, Yeats was considered Ireland's greatest poet – a title that has remained unchallenged. Just a few days before his death, he composed one of his last pieces of verse, his epitaph:

Cast a cold eye
On life, on death.
Horseman, pass by.

Constructive Unionism and the Home Rule Crisis

In the early years of the twentieth century, the question of Home Rule pulled Ireland apart.

After the fall of Parnell and the fracturing of Gladstone's Liberal party, Irish political unity foundered. The Conservatives claimed a strong majority in Westminster and adopted a new policy called 'Constructive Unionism', which was designed to kill by kindness the idea of Home Rule.

CONSTRUCTIVE UNIONISM

This policy was first employed by the Conservative Chief Secretary of Ireland, Arthur Balfour. Sometimes criticised for his strong-arm tactics, Balfour used public funds to build new railroads, which brought jobs to many and greatly increased the ability of rural farmers to sell their produce. Arthur was followed by his brother Gerald, who continued the policy, by reforming local politics to bring greater democracy and take power away from the landlords. He even opened up voting to women in these local elections.

In 1900, the job of Chief Secretary of Ireland passed to George Wyndham, who worked towards the elimination of the ongoing land issues. In 1902, a landowner named Captain John Shawe-Taylor invited the landlords and tenants, both Unionist and Nationalist, to a conference. In a rare display of solidarity, the convention concluded in favour of a massive government land purchase. Wyndham took the suggestion, and the 1903 Land Act became law. The Government made extremely generous offers to buy huge tracts of land, then broke up the land and sold the pieces at low-priced, fixed mortgages. The act proved so successful that, within a decade, the land issue that had haunted Ireland for centuries virtually disappeared.

ARTHUR BALFOUR (1848–1930)
The Conservative Chief Secretary of Ireland

HUGE TRACTS OF LAND
were broken up and sold at low-priced fixed mortgages

**HERBERT ASQUITH
(1852–1928)**
depicted here in a
caricature

By the time of the Land Act, the Irish Unionists in Parliament had reorganised themselves under John Redmond, but it was still several years before they made their voice heard. Their opportunity came in 1910, when a close election gave Redmond's Irish Parliamentary Party the deciding votes for government. The Irish returned the Liberals to power under Prime Minister Herbert Henry Asquith. The scene was set for a third attempt at a Home Rule bill.

The debate about Home Rule soon became tied up in the ongoing debate between the House of Commons and the House of Lords. For years, the Lords had been vetoing laws that many perceived to be in the best interests of the country. Supported by the Irish Parliamentary Party, Asquith forced through a constitutional reform. The Lords could still veto legislation, but only for two years running. If the House presented a bill for a third consecutive year, the Lords were forced to accept it.

Asquith now put forward a new Home Rule bill, to create an independent Irish Parliament to legislate domestic issues, with foreign issues still to be decided at Westminster. The bill passed through Commons, but was vetoed by the Lords.

This new Home Rule bill revealed the deep divisions between parts of Ulster and the rest of Ireland. In September 1912, the leader of the Ulster Unionists, Sir Edward Carson, organised a huge demonstration of almost 500,000 Ulster men and women, who signed a covenant to refuse Home Rule. The next year, the Unionists formed a militia, the Ulster Volunteer Force, which they secretly armed with imported weapons.

With civil war looming, and Asquith searching desperately for a compromise, the First World War erupted in Europe. The problems of Ireland were put on hold. The Home Rule bill became law on 18 September 1914, only to be immediately suspended for the duration of the war.

SIR EDWARD CARSON (1854–1935)
shown here in a political cartoon

Ireland in the First World War

Despite friction between Unionist and Nationalist parties in Ireland, both sides responded to Britain's call for manpower. Over 200,000 Irish fought in the Great War and nearly 30,000 died.

RECRUITMENT POSTER
Irishmen volunteered in their thousands during the Great War

YOUR FIRST DUTY IS TO TAKE YOUR PART IN ENDING THE WAR

JOIN AN IRISH REGIMENT TO-DAY

By August 1914, tension in Ireland had reached fever pitch. In less than two months, on 18 September, the Home Rule bill would be presented for the third consecutive year, and the House of Lords could do nothing to stop it. In the north of Ireland, Sir Edward Carson led Unionists in the formation of the Ulster Defence Force, an army willing to fight against Home Rule. In the south, Nationalists under John Redmond organised the Irish Volunteers in case of open conflict. On 3 August 1914, Germany invaded the neutral country of Belgium. The next day, the United Kingdom of Great Britain and Ireland declared war.

Edward Carson, showing his loyalty to the Union, immediately offered Britain the

36TH DIVISION

The 36th (Ulster) Division was composed entirely of men from the Ulster Defence Force, and Lord Kitchener even commissioned their officers. The 36th (Ulster) Division famously fought in the opening offensive at the Battle of the Somme in France, suffering nearly 5,000 casualties in the first two days. Later in the battle they ended up fighting side-by-side with the 16th (Irish) Division.

LORD KITCHENER (1850–1916) the Secretary for War had grown up in Ireland

services of the Ulster Defence Force. Meanwhile, John Redmond, worried that a lack of support might kill Home Rule, also pledged his Irish Volunteers to the fight. For the moment, the European war had prevented a civil war in Ireland. On 18 September 1914, Home Rule became law, but was suspended for one year or the duration of the war.

The displays of loyalty from both parts of Ireland were only begrudgingly accepted by the

British military. The Secretary for War, Lord Kitchener, who had grown up in Ireland, famously stated that he didn't trust any Irishman with a rifle in his hands.

In a war better known for its body count than its heroism, the Irish played their part with determination and loyalty, nearly completely filling out the 36th (Ulster), 16th (Irish) and 10th (Irish) Divisions.

It is almost certainly because of the sacrifice of these divisions that the 1916 Easter Rising in Dublin received so little immediate popular support, and the Irish continued to volunteer throughout

ROYAL IRISH RIFLES played their part in the Great War with determination and loyalty

10TH AND 16TH DIVISIONS

The Irish Volunteers were lumped into the 10th and 16th Divisions. In fact, these two Divisions were so predominantly Irish that they are often referred to as the 10th (Irish) and 16th (Irish) Divisions, but despite this, Lord Kitchener refused to allow them to display the Irish harp on their battle standards. The 10th (Irish) Division served at Gallipoli, before being sent to Salonika and Palestine. The 16th Division served on the Western Front.

the war. In 1918, the United Kingdom proposed the desperate idea of conscription in Ireland, but this suggestion was dropped after strong opposition from a coalition of the Catholic Church and nationalist Irish, led by Sinn Féin.

By the war's end in 1918, over 200,000 Irishmen had fought for the United Kingdom and around 30,000 had been killed. However, their sacrifice was, and continues to be, overshadowed by the revolutionaries of the Easter Rising. For many, Irish veterans fought the wrong war in the wrong place. The First World War may have temporarily obscured the conflicts within Ireland, but it did nothing to resolve them.

James Connolly

A socialist labour leader from Edinburgh, James Connolly played a major part in the Dublin Lockout before becoming the 'guiding brain' of the Easter Rising.

JAMES CONNOLLY (1868–1916) became the 'guiding brain' of the Easter Rising

Born in Edinburgh in 1868 to Irish immigrant parents, James Connolly grew up amidst the poverty of an exploited working class. His father earned a pittance carting manure, working long hours just to hold on to his job. In order to escape a similar fate, James left home, aged 14, and joined the British Army. Stationed in Ireland, he watched with growing horror as the Industrial Revolution drove thousands of people to the already overcrowded cities, especially Dublin and Belfast. Most lived in slums, with families of five or six living in a single room in houses that held upwards of 100 people. Meanwhile, unscrupulous employers, unbound by any kind of fair labour laws, took advantage of these desperate workers. These sights had a deep impact on the young James Connolly and,

KARL MARX (1818–1883)
whose works greatly influenced the young Connolly

OVERCROWDED CITIES saw many families living in slums

during his time in the army, he discovered the works of Karl Marx and eventually embraced socialism.

On leaving the army, Connolly became a socialist campaigner. In 1896, he established the Irish Socialist Republican Party in Dublin and became the founding editor of their newsletter, the *Workers' Republic*. However, Ireland was not ready for his socialist ideas, and by 1903 a burnt-out Connolly left for America. The time away re-energised Connolly, and in 1910 he returned to Ireland as the organiser of the Irish Transport and General Workers' Union in Belfast. Working closely with the Union's founder, James Larkin, Connolly helped conduct several successful union actions, and also founded the Irish Workers' Textile Union.

THE DUBLIN LOCKOUT

In 1913, James Larkin and James Connolly worked together in a bid for better pay for Dublin's tramway workers. When the United Tramway Company refused to work with the union, Larkin and Connolly organised a strike during the Dublin Horse Show, one of Ireland's most important events. The stand-off quickly escalated and became known as the Dublin Lockout. Soon, nearly 25,000 people were out of work, either striking or locked out. The authorities arrested both Larkin and Connolly, but this only made matters worse. At the highpoint of the dispute a large street battle erupted between police and protesters, leaving two people dead and hundreds wounded. Eventually, the strike failed. Larkin left Ireland for America, but Connolly struggled on.

After the Dublin Lockout, Connolly then helped organise the Irish Citizen Army – a small, but well-armed and well-drilled militia force, designed to protect workers from the violence of the police. This highly capable force attracted attention and in early 1916, the military council of the IRB invited Connolly and his army to join their planned rebellion. Although Connolly viewed the subject of Home Rule as secondary to workers' rights, he agreed to the alliance, and together they planned the Easter Rising.

JAMES LARKIN addressing the crowds at the Dublin Lockout

Because of his military background and his leadership of the Irish Citizen Army, the IRB handed military control of the rising to Connolly. In the words of Patrick Pearse, he became the 'guiding brain' of the rebellion. On 24 April 1916, Connolly led the rebels through the streets of Dublin to the General Post Office (GPO), where they set up their headquarters. For several days, he led the fight against the British army from the GPO until a bullet struck him in the leg. Badly wounded, Connolly refused to be evacuated, taking morphine to remain conscious until the rebels finally surrendered. On 12 May 1916, a firing squad executed Connolly as he sat in a chair, his wounded leg preventing him from standing.

Today, James Connolly is viewed as an Irish patriot, alongside the likes of Patrick Pearse. But ideologically he stood apart: he dreamed not of a free Ireland, but of an Ireland free of capitalist abuse.

KILMAINHAM PRISON
where Connolly was executed

Patrick Henry Pearse, Poet and Revolutionary

A poet and a revolutionary, Patrick Pearse proclaimed the formation of the Irish Republic at the beginning of the Easter Rising. Less than two weeks later, he died a martyr's death.

PATRICK PEARSE (1879–1916)
was a poet and revolutionary

'Ireland unfree shall never be at peace.'

When Patrick Henry Pearse spoke that line at the graveside of a noted Fenian bomber, he did so to stir the fires of revolution in the hearts of Irishmen. Pearse cleverly used his words as weapons against British Imperialism. He apparently feared neither death nor defeat, but only that his words and his cause might some day be forgotten.

A long-time supporter of Home Rule, Pearse believed that Ireland could never truly be free without the blood of revolution. In 1913, he helped found the Irish Volunteers, and soon after he joined the IRB, helping to control the Volunteers from the

THE EARLY YEARS

Born in Dublin in 1879 to an English father and an Irish mother, Pearse grew up with a rare perspective on the cause of Irish liberty. Aged eleven, he took up the study of the Irish language: its words and its ideals would drive him throughout his life. He studied law at university, but upon graduation decided to devote himself to the linked causes of Irish Nationalism and education. He wrote poetry both in English and Irish, often discussing the plight of Ireland. In 1903 he became the editor of An Claidheamh Soluis ('The Sword of Light'), the journal of the Gaelic League, and often lectured in Irish at Trinity College. In 1908, he helped to found St. Enda's, a boarding school for young men that infused the curriculum with the nobility of Irish culture. Above the doors to the school were inscribed the words of the greatest Irish hero, Cú Chulainn: 'I care not though I were to live but one day and one night, if only my fame and my deeds live after me'.

GAELIC WARRIORS
such as Cúchulainn
inspired Pearse in his
nationalist quest

inside. As the First World War captured the attention and caused a fracture in the Irish Volunteers, Pearse used his gift as an orator and a writer to shift the ideology of the Irish Volunteers from a defence of Home Rule to a revolutionary force.

POBLACHT NA H EIREANN.

THE PROVISIONAL GOVERNMENT
OF THE
IRISH REPUBLIC
TO THE PEOPLE OF IRELAND.

IRISHMEN AND IRISHWOMEN: In the name of God and of the dead generations from which she receives her old tradition of nationhood, Ireland, through us, summons her children to her flag and strikes for her freedom.

Having organised and trained her manhood through her secret revolutionary organisation, the Irish Republican Brotherhood, and through her open military organisations, the Irish Volunteers and the Irish Citizen Army, having patiently perfected her discipline, having resolutely waited for the right moment to reveal itself, she now seizes that moment, and, supported by her exiled children in America and by gallant allies in Europe, but relying in the first on her own strength, she strikes in full confidence of victory.

We declare the right of the people of Ireland to the ownership of Ireland, and to the unfettered control of Irish destinies, to be sovereign and indefeasible. The long usurpation of that right by a foreign people and government has not extinguished the right, nor can it ever be extinguished except by the destruction of the Irish people. In every generation the Irish people have asserted their right to national freedom and sovereignty; six times during the past three hundred years they have asserted it in arms. Standing on that fundamental right and again asserting it in arms in the face of the world, we hereby proclaim the Irish Republic as a Sovereign Independent State, and we pledge our lives and the lives of our comrades-in-arms to the cause of its freedom, of its welfare, and of its exaltation among the nations.

The Irish Republic is entitled to, and hereby claims, the allegiance of every Irishman and Irishwoman. The Republic guarantees religious and civil liberty, equal rights and equal opportunities to all its citizens, and declares its resolve to pursue the happiness and prosperity of the whole nation and of all its parts, cherishing all the children of the nation equally, and oblivious of the differences carefully fostered by an alien government, which have divided a minority from the majority in the past.

Until our arms have brought the opportune moment for the establishment of a permanent National Government, representative of the whole people of Ireland and elected by the suffrages of all her men and women, the Provisional Government, hereby constituted, will administer the civil and military affairs of the Republic in trust for the people.

We place the cause of the Irish Republic under the protection of the Most High God, Whose blessing we invoke upon our arms, and we pray that no one who serves that cause will dishonour it by cowardice, inhumanity, or rapine. In this supreme hour the Irish nation must, by its valour and discipline and by the readiness of its children to sacrifice themselves for the common good, prove itself worthy of the august destiny to which it is called.

Signed on behalf of the Provisional Government,
THOMAS J. CLARKE.
SEAN Mac DIARMADA,   THOMAS MacDONAGH,
P. H. PEARSE,   EAMONN CEANNT,
JAMES CONNOLLY.   JOSEPH PLUNKETT.

THE PROCLAMATION
of the Irish Republic
was read aloud on
the steps of the
General Post Office

When the revolution finally came in Easter week of 1916, Pearse marched at the head of the column of troops that seized the General Post Office. He then stood on the post office steps and read aloud the Proclamation of the Irish Republic that he had signed and helped to draft.

'Irishmen and Irishwomen: In the name of God and of the dead generation from which she receives her old tradition of nationhood, Ireland, through us, summons her children to her flag and strikes for her freedom...'

In his position as President of the Irish Republic, it is likely that Pearse knew that the rising could not succeed. Still, for five days, apparently without sleep, he led his revolutionaries with the power of his words and helped drive them in their defiance. Then, with

Dublin burning around him, he negotiated the new Irish surrender in order to prevent more damage to the civilian population.

For the leaders of the Easter Rising, surrender meant certain execution, and Pearse knew it. He faced the firing squad on 3 May 1916. Before he died, he wrote a letter to his mother, in which he said: 'This is the death I should have asked for if God had given me the choice of all deaths – to die a soldier's death for Ireland and for Freedom'.

THE GENERAL POST Office in Dublin, depicted here before the destruction caused by the Easter Rising

The Easter Rising

During Easter week in 1916, Dublin became a battlefield, as the Irish Volunteers and Irish Citizen Army fought against the British in a doomed attempt to establish the Irish Republic.

By 1916, the citizens and officials of Dublin had grown used to the men of the Irish Volunteers marching and parading through the streets in defence of Home Rule. Led by the popular, and seemingly peaceful, Professor Eoin MacNeill, the British authorities generally allowed the militia group to do as they pleased. However, unbeknownst to nearly everyone, including MacNeill, the Irish Volunteers had been infiltrated by the radical core of the Irish Republican Brotherhood. Led by the articulate and persuasive Patrick Pearse, the IRB took control of the operations of the Irish Volunteers and began plotting rebellion.

The main impediment to the planned uprising was a lack of weapons. While the IRB used legal and illegal means to obtain small arms, they soon sought help from Britain's wartime enemy. After long and complicated negotiations, the Germans agreed to send a shipment of weapons to Ireland to aid in the rebellion. The IRB also formed an alliance with James Connolly and his small, but well-trained and well-equipped, Irish Citizen Army. With all the pieces in place, the uprising was scheduled for 23 April; Easter Sunday.

The first day of the Rising was marked by confusion as the rebels took control of parts of the

EAMON CEANNT (1881–1916) was a republican who served on the IRB's Supreme Council

SATURDAY, 22 APRIL

Just one day before the planned rising, disaster struck the conspirators. The Royal Navy intercepted the Aud, the German vessel carrying weapons to the rebels. To avoid capture, the captain sank his ship, and it went down along with thousands of rifles. Around the same time, Eoin MacNeill discovered the conspiracy and the planned rising. He immediately dispatched messages to the Irish Volunteers that all Easter manoeuvres had been cancelled. The rebellion was called off.

THOMAS CLARKE (1857–1916) was a member of the IRB'S Military Council and was executed after the Rising

SUNDAY, 23 APRIL

On Easter Sunday, the conspirators met and made a fateful decision. Patrick Pearse, along with James Connolly, Tom Clarke, Sean MacDermott, Joseph Plunkett, Thomas MacDonagh and Eamon Ceannt, elected to reschedule the Rising for the next day. Most probably knew that such a rising could not succeed with so little organisation and no idea of numbers, but they accepted their fate and went their separate ways to prepare for rebellion.

**JOSEPH PLUNKETT
(1887–1916)**
was a poet and revolutionary who directed military operations for the Rising

MONDAY, 24 APRIL

On Easter Monday, around 1,200 members of the Irish Volunteers and Irish Citizen Army met around Dublin. They then marched to strategic buildings and roads around the city and seized control. The leadership of the Rising occupied the General Post Office in the heart of the city and, from its steps, Patrick Pearse announced the formation of the Irish Republic. His proclamation was met with amused indifference.

city; however, the British army soon responded with overwhelming force. The rebels used surprise and area knowledge to win a few skirmishes, but they were no match for the firepower of the British. While infantry and machine-gunners duelled in the city streets, long-range artillery blasted the rebel positions to pieces, and raging fires spread through the city. By 29 April, Patrick Pearse decided to surrender, to save Dublin from further harm.

Public opinion seemed to favour the British before and during the Rising, but it soon shifted in the aftermath. Stories of a mass murder by British troops and unwarranted executions turned the Irish against the army. The main conspirators were tried in closed court-martial and condemned to death by firing squad. It would not be long before these men were viewed as martyrs.

GENERAL POST OFFICE
during the Rising

Sinn Féin and the First Dáil

A political group that rose to prominence in Ireland during the First World War, Sinn Féin took virtual control of the country by establishing the First Dáil in 1919.

In the wake of the chaos and destruction of the Easter Rising, many in the British and Irish press mislabelled the event the 'Sinn Féin Rising'. Although the non-violent Sinn Féin had taken no part in either the planning or execution of the Rising, the name stuck in the public consciousness and it had a profound result on Irish politics following the First World War.

DUBLIN
following the destruction of the Easter Rising

In 1914, Sinn Féin organised an anti-recruitment campaign against the British army and thereby became a rallying point for pacifists and anti-war demonstrators. This campaign may have caused the press to confuse Sinn Féin with the secretive Irish Republican

Brotherhood, who had actually engineered the Easter Rising. The mix-up caused a huge surge of membership into Sinn Féin after the execution of the leaders of the Easter Rising. With a new radical element flooding the organisation, a party convention was called in October of 1917. At this meeting, Arthur Griffith stood down as president in favour of Eamon de Valera.

AIMS OF SINN FÉIN

Founded in 1905 by Arthur Griffith and Bulmer Hobson, Sinn Féin collected together a number of smaller radical political groups, including disenchanted Fenians and Nationalists, as well as pacifists and feminists. Literally translated, the name means 'ourselves' or 'we ourselves', but 'ourselves alone' has also been used. The organisation stated its main goal as the establishment of an independent Irish Republic under the monarch and advocated a policy of passive resistance to achieve its aims. Most notably, it pushed for Irish MPs to withdraw from Westminster and establish a ruling council in Ireland, and for Irish citizens to forgo British institutions such as courts in favour of Irish equivalents. The group made little headway in its first decade of existence, but that all changed with the outbreak of the First World War.

Arthur Griffith

**EAMON DE VALERA
(1882–1975)**
became a national
hero and leader of
Sinn Féin

An Irish-American, Eamon de Valera had been one of the leaders of the Easter Rising and only escaped execution because of his dual citizenship and the intervention of the American ambassador. As the highest-ranking of the revolutionaries to survive, de Valera became a national hero, and an obvious choice to lead Sinn Féin. Under de Valera, the organisation led the protests against British conscription in 1918. When Britain unjustly arrested most of the organisation's leadership for conspiring with the Germans, it unwittingly confirmed Sinn Féin as the Nationalist Party of Ireland. In the election later that year, Sinn Féin captured 73 of Ireland's 105 parliamentary seats.

The rise of Sinn Féin further highlighted the division between the north and the south of Ireland. After the election, the Sinn Féin MPs refused to take their seats in Westminster. Instead, they invited all Irish MPs to form the first Dáil in Dublin in January 1919. In the event, only the Sinn Féin members attended, and only half of those, as the other half were still in prison. Despite this poor representation, the Dáil set about

THE FIRST DÁIL
met in Dublin
in 1919

forming the government for a new, independent Irish
Republic, based upon the proclamation of the Easter
Rising, with Eamon de Valera as the new president. But,
even as the Dáil held its first meetings in Dublin, the
first shots of the Anglo-Irish war were fired.

THE RISE
of Sinn Féin further
highlighted the
division between
north and south

As the entire country descended into violence, Sinn
Féin and the Dáil increasingly took a political back seat
to the Irish Republican Army. Although the names of
Sinn Féin and the Dáil have survived to
the present, both organisations
are, at best, indirectly descended
from those that existed in the
first quarter of the twentieth
century.

The Birth of the Irish Republican Army

Born from the remains of the Irish Volunteers, the Irish Republican Army fought against British rule using terror, intimidation and guerrilla tactics.

CATHAL BRUGHA (1874–1922) was named as the Minister of Defence of the new Irish Republic

When British forces executed the leaders of the Easter Rising in 1916, their leniency towards the rest of the Irish Volunteers left the organisation relatively intact. By 1917, the Irish Volunteers had reorganised under new leadership. Outlawed and prohibited from openly marching or training, the group went underground to continue to rearm and plot their next move. However, when Eamon de Valera and Sinn Féin established the First Dáil in early 1919, one of the Irish Volunteer leaders, Cathal Brugha, was named as the Minister of Defence of the new Irish

Republic. Many of the Irish, and especially the press, assumed that the Irish Volunteers would become the official standing army of the new republic and began referring to the Irish Volunteers as the Irish Republican Army (IRA). However, the truth of the situation was much more complicated.

Despite the prominent positions of Irish Volunteer leaders such as Brugha and even de Valera, no official connection between the Irish Volunteers and Sinn Féin existed. The Irish Volunteers had purposely maintained a decentralised structure that allowed each cell a great deal of autonomy. Some parts of the Irish Volunteers embraced their new status as the IRA, others did not. To make matters even more confusing, many Irish Volunteer cells were still under the control of the secretive and militant Irish Republican Brotherhood. While the Dáil began its debate on how to achieve separation from Britain, one group of Irish Volunteers went on the offensive.

VIOLENCE BEGINS

On 21 January 1919, a group of nine Irish Volunteers ambushed a pair of popular local policemen at Soloheadbeg in County Tipperary. The Volunteers called upon the police to surrender, but then shot both men dead at point blank range before they could reply. This brutal act of murder set off the Anglo-Irish War, one of the most confusing and indiscriminately violent conflicts in the history of both Ireland and Britain. Although the IRA probably had less than 3,000 armed men, they launched a campaign of terror that swept across the island. They began by targeting the uniformed members of the Royal Irish Constabulary, murdering them on city streets, in their cars and even dragging them from their beds. Soon, anyone associated with British authority or rule became a legitimate target. When the IRA wanted to make an example of a British sympathiser, they would often shoot them in the thigh or kneecap, crippling them for life. The IRA buried one man in the sand by the sea and left him to drown in the incoming tide. The IRA proved to have little or no guilt about any level of cruelty and would happily murder a British soldier or police officer in front of his wife or children.

The Third Tipperary Brigade flying column, during the Anglo-Irish War

**MICHAEL COLLINS
(1890–1922)**
became the new
leader of the Irish
Republican Army

During this reign of terror, the Irish Republican Army found a new leader from the ranks of the Irish Republican Brotherhood, named Michael Collins. Already the Minister of Finance in the new Irish Republic, Michael Collins proved a brilliant organiser who understood the power of terror. While directing the various cells in the campaign that now included burning police barracks and tax offices across the country, Collins recruited the most callous, brutal and efficient members of the IRA into a special assassination group called 'The Squad'. The Squad went after high-profile targets, including detectives and high-ranking civil servants.

As the violence continued to spread out of control, Britain made a terrible mistake. Instead of appealing to the vast majority of the Irish who dreamed of peace, the government in Westminster sent over a new volunteer police force in order to confront the IRA. Dressed in a hodgepodge of Black and Tan uniforms, this new force matched the IRA atrocity for atrocity.

The Black and Tans &
the First Bloody Sunday

As the violence and terrorism of the Irish War of
Independence dragged on into a second year, the
British responded by sending over ex-soldiers to
help the Royal Irish Constabulary. Called the Black
and Tans and Auxiliaries, they proved just as
adept at brutality as the Irish Republican Army.

**ROYAL IRISH
CONSTABULARY**
(RIC) badge

Irish history books, including this one, date the
outbreak of this Irish War of Independence as 21
January 1919. However, this date was applied later.
At the time, many people, especially in Britain, were
slow to realise that the problems in Ireland amounted
to a full-blown war. The Irish Republican Army was
not an army in the classical sense. It had no uniforms,
nor a strong command structure. It did not move or
march in formation, nor did it attempt to capture
territory. But, under the direction of Michael Collins,
the IRA did pursue an organised campaign of

assassination and terror, designed to drive the British out of Ireland. It was a guerrilla war, more akin to the modern conflict in Afghanistan than to either of the World Wars.

WAR VETERANS applied for work in Ireland

For nearly a year, the actions of the IRA paralysed the British administration. Although the Royal Irish Constabulary (RIC) did its best to maintain law and order, it suffered badly at the hands of an enemy it could not distinguish from the people it was supposed to protect. The numbers of the RIC dwindled as casualties and resignations took their toll. Finally, Britain awoke to the desperation of the situation. Unable to recruit the necessary numbers of police in Ireland, Britain offered ten shillings a day to anyone who would go to Ireland and try to keep the peace. Thousands volunteered, including numerous First World War veterans who had been unable to find work or readjust to civilian life after the horrors of the trenches.

Britain began shipping these new recruits to
Ireland in early 1920. At first there were not enough
RIC uniforms for the men, and they ended up wearing
a mixture of dark green coats, black belts and tan

BLOODY SUNDAY

On 21 November 1920, the two forces
reached new heights of cruelty in a day
of violence known as 'Bloody Sunday'. It
began when Michael Collins ordered the

murder of a number of suspected British
intelligence agents. Members of his 'Squad'
broke into homes, shot dead 13 men and
wounded another six. In response, the RIC
shot a pair of IRA prisoners 'while trying
to escape'. Then, RIC Auxiliaries went to a
crowded Gaelic football match in Dublin in
order to search for suspects. What happened
next is still debated, but at some point
the Auxiliaries opened fire. Twelve people
were killed, including one of the players, a
woman and a child. Another 60 people
were wounded.

Croke Park in Dublin was the
scene of a terrible atrocity

or khaki trousers. The Irish soon labelled these new recruits 'Black and Tans', a name borrowed from a famous pack of Irish hounds.

The Black and Tans made their presence felt in Ireland almost immediately. Unbound by strict military discipline, hardened to violence by the horrors of the Great War and possessing no connection to or love for Ireland, the Black and Tans proved a match for the IRA in inflicting violence and terror. The war quickly developed a pattern of cold, clinical assassination by the IRA, followed by swift, indiscriminate reprisals by the Black and Tans. If a police constable was murdered, the Black and Tans and Auxiliaries would ride through the town shooting through windows and setting houses on fire. They attacked and often murdered anyone known to have Sinn Féin connections.

The slaughter of Bloody Sunday, as well as other atrocities committed by the Black and Tans, caused outrage and embarrassment back in Britain. Now fully conscious that Britain was at war in Ireland, the government desperately searched for a way to end it.

The Anglo-Irish Treaty

After two and a half years of conflict, the Anglo-Irish War finally ended with the signing of the controversial Anglo-Irish Treaty.

LLOYD GEORGE (1863–1945) was desperate to find a solution to the Irish problem

After the horrors of Bloody Sunday, the violence in Ireland escalated once again. The IRA formed 'flying columns' of 35 or more armed men that would lay

ambushes for RIC convoys. The Black and Tans and other British forces continued to take reprisals on the populace, including burning down a large section of Cork. Both sides were strained to the limit. Over 500 police and military had been killed along with a greater number of IRA members and civilians. Even the cool and calculating Michael Collins wondered how much longer he could hold his forces together.

In Britain, the government, under Prime Minister Lloyd George, desperately sought a solution. In December 1920, it proposed the Government of Ireland Act which revived the idea of Home Rule, but divided Ireland into two pieces. The six Protestant counties of Northern Ireland would form one unit; the rest of Ireland the other. Both units would have their own internal parliament to decide domestic issues. With most of the Irish seats in the Westminster parliament belonging to the absent Sinn Féin, the act passed easily. However, it had little immediate effect. While the violence between the IRA and the RIC continued in the south, a small civil war had developed in the north between the Catholics and Protestants. Belfast became a battleground, as disorganised gangs fought bloody skirmishes in the streets.

GEORGE V (1865–1936) travelled to Ireland for the opening of the new Northern Ireland Parliament

Then, King George V made a bold and brave decision. Against the advice of many, he decided to travel to Belfast for the opening of the new Northern Ireland Parliament. Although the dozen Sinn Féin and

Nationalist MPs refused to attend, the King rose before the 40 Unionist MPs and gave a speech addressed to all Irishmen. He said: 'I appeal to all Irishmen to pause… and join in making for the land which they love a new era of peace, contentment and good will.' The King's speech echoed across the island, repeated in newspapers and from mouth to mouth. A few weeks later, a truce was called.

With the guns momentarily silent, Eamon de Valera agreed to send a delegation to London to work out a lasting peace. For reasons that are still unclear, de Valera declined to go himself and instead sent a team led by Arthur Griffith and Michael Collins, with orders to accept only a treaty that included either a full break from the British Empire or full unity for Ireland. In the end, the Irish got neither.

SIGNING
of the Anglo-Irish
Treaty in 1921

THE ANGLO-IRISH TREATY

A team from Britain, led by Lloyd George and including Winston Churchill, debated the issue with the Irish representatives for nearly two months. Exasperated, Lloyd George finally offered the Irish an ultimatum: sign the treaty as it stood at that moment or face a resumption of war. On December 6 1921, Arthur Griffith, Michael Collins and the other Irish delegates signed the Anglo-Irish Treaty, which established the Irish Free State as a dominion of the British Empire. The North of Ireland would be given the option of joining the Free State or remaining independent. In the latter case, a special 'Boundary Commission' would be established to redraw the border between the two states.

Winston Churchill
(1874-1965)

When Griffith and Collins returned to Ireland they were blasted by de Valera and other Irish Nationalists. For most, the division of Ireland was less important than the fact that the Irish would still be required to make an oath to the King. Despite de Valera's objection, the Dáil ratified the treaty. The Anglo-Irish War was over, but the divisions left in its wake would soon tear Ireland apart.

The Irish Civil War

Despite the ratification of the Anglo-Irish Treaty, many within the IRA refused to accept its terms and plunged Ireland into a brief civil war.

MAP OF IRELAND
showing the Irish
Free State

By all rights, 1921 should have been a glorious year for Ireland. The Anglo-Irish Treaty had granted Ireland dominion status, and thus a separate parliament largely to regulate its own affairs. The United Kingdom of Great Britain and Ireland was no more, and the new Irish Free State had been born. However, for many who had fought in the brutal war for independence, it was not enough. When Arthur Griffith and Michael Collins returned from London with the treaty, many within Sinn Féin and the Irish Republican Army declared the two men traitors, and once again vowed to take up arms and fight until Ireland was fully free of the British Empire.

The first battle occurred within the Dáil, where republican forces led by Eamon de Valera argued against acceptance of the treaty. In a nasty debate that hinged mainly on semantics, the treaty was ratified(passed). De Valera resigned, and Arthur Griffith became the new head of the Dáil. Since Britain didn't recognise the Dáil as an official body, the Irish set up a new provisional government with Michael Collins as the chairman. The British handed over Dublin castle to the new government and left the island, but any jubilation the Irish might have felt was tempered by the looming threat of the IRA.

THE FLAG OF IRELAND contains both green and orange to symbolise the unification of Protestants and Catholics

**LIAM LYNCH
(1893–1923)**
led irregulars in
a guerrilla war

Despite his many years as its leader, Michael Collins had no true authority over the IRA. Because of its decentralised nature, individual groups made their own political decisions, and most decided to fight against the treaty. For several months, a tense stand-off occurred. The IRA, often called 'irregulars' during this period, took control of several prominent Dublin buildings, including the Four Corners. Meanwhile, Michael Collins built up a new Free State Army with help from the British. The standoff came to a head on 22 June 1922, when IRA gunmen murdered Field Marshall Sir Henry Wilson outside his house in London. The British demanded that Collins deal with the IRA, or the treaty would be revoked.

Trapped between fighting his former allies or resuming the war with Britain, Collins surrounded the IRA strongholds in Dublin and called on the irregulars to surrender. When they refused, he opened fire. In many ways, the opening shots of the Irish Civil War mirrored the Easter Rising, but this time Irishman fought Irishman. Collins's better trained and better organised troops quickly eliminated the threat inside Dublin and other major cities. The irregulars retreated into the mountains and, under the leadership of Liam Lynch, fought a guerrilla war similar to their fight in the Anglo-Irish War.

THE CUSTOMS HOUSE in Dublin was badly burned by an IRA attack in 1921

Unlike the previous war, however, the IRA received little support from the general populace. Tired by years of conflict, most Irish longed for peace and backed the forces of the new Free State. Slowly, the various irregular cells were isolated and destroyed. In April of 1923, Liam Lynch was cornered and killed. His death signalled the end of the conflict. On 30 April, the soldiers of the IRA threw down their arms and melted away.

Unlike most civil wars, the Irish conflict was not about a deep ideological divide among the population. Instead, it was created and maintained by the passions of a few powerful individuals. Nearly 1,000 people died during the Irish Civil War, including the first chairman of a Free Irish State, Michael Collins.

The Death of Michael Collins

Considered by some to be the greatest Irish hero since Brian Bórú, Michael Collins lived and died in the name of a free Irish State.

After signing his name to the 1921 Anglo-Irish Treaty, Michael Collins stated that he had signed his own death warrant. Collins knew that many Irish would not receive the treaty well, but he believed that it gave Ireland the best possible chance to achieve eventually full independent statehood, a cause that Collins had spent most of his life fighting to obtain.

LONDON
where Michael Collins took a job with the Post Office

By 1915, Collins had risen in the ranks of the IRB, and possibly helped in the planning and preparation for the Easter Rising. When the Rising finally came, Michael Collins fought alongside Patrick Pearse and James Connolly in the General Post Office. Spared from execution because of his seemingly low rank within the Irish Volunteers, Collins spent a short

MICHAEL COLLINS

Born the youngest of eight children in County Cork in 1890, Michael Collins grew up in a staunchly republican household. His father had been a member of the Fenians and passed his ideals on to his children. After leaving school at the age of 15, Collins travelled to London and took a job working for the Post Office. During this time, Collins became involved with the Irish Republican Brotherhood, and he quickly rose through its ranks.

time in prison. Although held as an Irish hero by most people, Collins considered the Easter Rising a bitter and mostly pointless failure. He realised that the Irish could never hope to defeat the British if they allowed themselves to be hemmed in and trapped.

After his release from prison, Michael Collins joined Sinn Féin and won the election as MP for South Cork. Refusing to take his seat in Westminster, he instead joined the rest of Sinn Féin in forming the First Dáil and landed the position of Minister of Finance and Home Affairs. By this point, Michael Collins had also become one of the leaders of the IRB.

MICHAEL COLLINS
quickly rose through
the ranks of the IRB

Although it is doubtful that he had a direct hand
in starting the Anglo-Irish War, he quickly embraced
the conflict. While it is still debated exactly how much
control Collins had over the IRA, he certainly controlled
a number of elements in and around Dublin, including
his 'squad' of special assassins. He also possessed a
tremendous intelligence network that allowed him to
find targets of opportunity.

Cold, calculating and ruthless, Collins showed
little pity as he waged his war against the British.
Despite a lack of resources, Collins used his natural
organisational ability to drive the British to breaking
point. When the British finally called for a
truce, Collins reluctantly agreed to
serve as an Irish representative to
the treaty talks.

Upon returning to Ireland
with the treaty, the new
government of the Irish Free
State elected Collins as its first
chairman. In this position,

THE DEATH OF
Michael Collins on
22 August 1922

he led the battle against the IRA republicans who threatened to reduce his fledgling state to anarchy.

On 22 August 1922, Michael Collins was returning from an inspection tour when a group of IRA gunmen ambushed his convoy. Instead of driving through the ambush, Collins ordered his men to get out and fire back. During the fire fight, a bullet tore through Collins's skull, killing him instantly. Collins's men managed to return his body to Dublin, where it lay in state for three days in Dublin City Hall. Tens of thousands of mourners paid their respects.

Today, Michael Collins is an almost mythical figure in Irish history. To some, he is the greatest hero since Brian Bóru, and his death was a tragedy without equal. Others see him as a ruthless patriot, whose single-minded devotion greatly advanced the cause of Irish statehood.

MICHAEL COLLINS'S body lay in state in Dublin for three days

Partition

With the signing of the Anglo-Irish Treaty in 1921, Ireland split into two states – the Irish Free State and Northern Ireland. Within a few years, this separation had become permanent.

Around the time of the Ulster Plantation, wave upon wave of Scottish immigrants settled in the north of Ireland, bringing with them a hard work ethic, a Presbyterian faith and a support of the union of Ireland and Great Britain. As the years passed, wars, rebellion, terrorism and business combined to increase the British presence in Ulster at the expense of the native Irish. By the dawn of the twentieth century, it had become clear that several counties within Ulster considered themselves more British than Irish, and were prepared to fight to remain part of the United Kingdom.

POLITICAL CARTOON showing the Ulster pig walking away from the Home Rule pen

When the question of Home Rule arose again in 1912, one British MP proposed that any new Home Rule Bill should not apply to the counties of Antrim, Armagh, Down or Londonderry. Within a few years, the debate centred on the question of whether a separate Northern Ireland should be composed of six or nine counties and whether this division should become permanent. As the debate raged, Ulster armed itself, forming the Ulster Volunteers, and bringing Ireland to the brink of civil war. Then the First World War intervened. Home Rule was suspended and the question of partition temporarily dropped.

As the Great War ended, Ireland quickly descended into the chaos of the Anglo-Irish War. In the north, this became a local civil war as the Protestants seized the opportunity to try to drive their Catholic neighbours out, and the Catholics fought back just as hard. In 1920, the British Parliament passed the Government of Ireland Act in an effort to stop the war. This bill created a separate Northern Ireland, consisting of the four counties listed above, plus Fermanagh and Tyrone.

WORLD WAR I
delayed the question of Home Rule and partition for four years

POLITICAL CARTOON
displaying a divided
peace for Ireland

In truth, this bill had little meaning until the negotiations for the Anglo-Irish Treaty. In order to end hostilities, the Irish representatives had to accept the partition, provided that a 'Boundary Commission' would examine the partition and redraw the border based upon religious and cultural lines. Almost immediately upon accepting the treaty, the Irish Republican Army began using terrorism to attack the Protestant infrastructure in the north.

The attacks didn't last, however. As the Irish Free State fell into civil war, IRA forces concentrated their efforts in the south, giving Northern Ireland a chance to consolidate and organise. By the time the Irish Civil War ended, Northern Ireland stood as the more stable of the two states on the island.

Finally, in late 1924, the Boundary Commission went to work, with Eoin MacNeill representing the Irish Free State, and J. R. Fisher standing for Northern Ireland. Although the Commission discovered that much of the populace in some parts of Northern

Ireland still considered themselves staunchly Irish, a clause in the treaty stated that Northern Ireland had to remain an economically viable state. Eventually, the Commission collapsed, after its findings were leaked to the press. In the end, in order to keep peace and prevent the outbreak of yet another conflict, the governments of the United Kingdom, Northern Ireland and the Irish Free State signed a three-way agreement in 1925, confirming the border as it stood.

Since 1925, Northern Ireland has remained separate from the rest of Ireland and has also retained a place in the United Kingdom. The debate continues to the present day, and many within the Republic of Ireland still see reunification as one of the major goals of government.

NORTHERN IRELAND has remained separate from the rest of Ireland

Fianna Fáil and the Irish Constitution

In the years following the Civil War, Eamon de Valera fashioned a new political party that would dominate Irish politics for most of the twentieth century and write Ireland's new constitution.

WILLIAM COSGRAVE (1880–1965) took over the leadership of the Irish Free State

With the deaths of Arthur Griffith and Michael Collins in 1922, leadership of the Irish Free State passed to William Cosgrave – a former Volunteer who had fought in the Easter Rising. In 1923, Cosgrave formed a new political party named Cumann na nGaedheal, 'the party of the Irish', in order to support the democracy established under the Anglo-Irish treaty. Later that year, Cosgrave called for the first general election in the Irish Free State. Cumann na nGaedheal won the vote, edging out de Valera's Sinn Féin.

Still considered a hero by many for his leadership in the Easter Rising, Eamon de Valera broke away from Sinn Féin and formed his own political party, Fianna

REBUILDING

For ten years, William Cosgrave led Ireland in a period of slow, careful rebuilding. One of his major projects was the building of the great hydro-electric dam across the river Shannon, which would supply most of the country's electric power for years to come. However, when the great depression struck Ireland in 1932, many in Ireland grew tired of his slow policies and called for a change. In the general election held that year, Éamon de Valera once again came to the forefront of Irish politics.

Fianna Fáil, led by de Valera, won the elections in 1932

Fáil, meaning 'Warriors of Ireland'. Composed of large chunks of former Sinn Féin supporters and less radical anti-treaty voters, Fianna Fáil won 72 seats in the 1932 election and formed a new government, with de Valera at its head.

Taking advantage of many of the policies enacted by Cosgrave, de Valera led Ireland in a period of radical restructuring and separation from Great Britain. His first act was to abolish the Oath of Allegiance to the British crown, which had formerly kept members of Sinn Féin from taking their seats in Parliament. Then, in 1935, de Valera set a group of civil servants the task of constructing a new Irish Constitution to guide the country towards full independence. In 1937, Eamon de Valera presented the Constitution to the people and called for a popular vote. With a vote of 645,105 for the Constitution and 526,945 against it, the bill passed and became law in December of 1937.

Since its adoption in 1937, the Constitution has undergone many changes and challenges, but remains the fundamental basis for Irish Government. More importantly, for the southern 26 counties, it brought about the final end to over 500 years of British government intervention in Ireland.

THE NEW CONSTITUTION

Although the new Constitution was built on the foundation of the older 1922 Free State Constitution, it contained a number of important differences. First and foremost, it gave the country a new name, Éire (or Ireland in English), and declared the country as a sovereign and independent state. It defined Éire as consisting of the entire island of Ireland, but recognised that its authority, temporarily, only extended to the southern 26 counties. The Constitution also replaced the position of Prime Minster with a new, more powerful head of government called the Taoiseach, derived from the ancient Irish word for king or chief. Ireland also gained a President, to serve as the head of state, who would wield far-reaching discretionary powers.

In a move that angered many of the remnants of the old Protestant Ascendancy, the Constitution also accorded a special position to the Catholic Church, and adopted many of its teachings as law. The sale of contraceptives was outlawed and divorce would henceforth be made illegal.

Finally, the Constitution did much to ensure the survival and rebirth of Irish language and culture. The study of Irish became a mandatory part of childhood education, and fluency became a requirement for work in civil service. All government documents were produced in both Irish and English.

Irish harp

Road signs were written in both English and Irish

Ireland in the Second World War

Despite Eamon de Valera's declaration that Ireland would remain neutral during World War II, the country did much to support the Allied cause. Meanwhile, Northern Ireland once again proved her loyalty and devotion to the Union.

WINSTON CHURCHILL (opposite) offered to support reunification of Ireland

RECRUITMENT (below) of 50,000 Irishmen aided Britain in the war

As far back as the 1903 Land Act, Irish farmers had borrowed money from the British government in order to buy land. However, soon after Eamon de Valera came to power, he put a stop to the repayment of these loans. Incensed, the British responded by placing a 20% tax on a majority of Irish imports. For the next six years, the two governments went back and forth, replying tit for tat in a feud called the 'Economic War'. Finally, in 1938, the Irish Government paid the British ten million pounds to settle their differences and to end the British occupation of the 'treaty ports' (naval military bases used by Britain under the terms of the Anglo-Irish Treaty). For a moment, the relations between the two countries stabilised, but soon, Britain would have cause to regret giving up the treaty ports. In 1939, Britain declared war on Nazi Germany.

Although Ireland had little love for the fascist regimes of the Axis powers, de Valera had based his entire political career on a complete separation from Britain. In a move that has since caused great controversy and debate, de Valera declared that Ireland would remain neutral in the conflict. Even when Prime Minister Winston Churchill later offered to support reunification of Ireland in return for an alliance, de Valera stuck to his guns and proved, once and for all, that Ireland would decide her own destiny. However, the truth of de Valera's 'neutrality' was not quite as unbiased as the word might imply.

HELP AT SEA

On the same day that Ireland declared neutrality, a storm forced a British military seaplane to land in the sea near Dublin. The Irish immediately gave assistance to the plane crew, then allowed them to buy fuel and fly away. Quickly and quietly, the Irish adopted a policy of helping downed Allied airmen and sending them back to Britain or to Northern Ireland. On the other hand, downed Axis airmen were interned for the duration of the war. Ireland also passed along intercepted German messages, as well as advance weather reports to Britain.

HELP AT SEA
was given by the
Irish to Allied airmen

As well as its assistance for downed airmen, Ireland's biggest support came when it made no effort to stop its populace from volunteering to aid the British. During the length of the war, over 200,000 Irish went to work in Britain, filling a gaping hole in the British economy left by the men who had gone off to fight. In addition, nearly 50,000 Irishmen volunteered to fight for Britain, earning hundreds of battle honours and seven Victoria Crosses (the United Kingdom's highest military award).

THE VICTORIA CROSS
was awarded to
seven Irishmen in
recognition of their
bravery in the war

While Ireland practised a lopsided neutrality, Northern Ireland once again proved her loyalty to the United Kingdom. Despite having very limited military capabilities, several key airfields were built in Northern Ireland, and Londonderry became a key port for the Atlantic Convoys that moved supplies from the United States to Britain. The north suffered for its loyalty, however. In 1941, the 'Belfast Blitz' saw German bombers destroy 56,000 homes and kill approximately 1,000 people in air-raids. From 1942, the United States took over the defence of Northern Ireland and used it as a base to plan the Invasion of North Africa and to build up troops for D-Day. In all, over 300,000 United States servicemen were stationed in Northern Ireland during the war.

In retrospect, Ireland has little to be ashamed of in its war record. Northern Ireland gave every assistance it could to help protect the United Kingdom and to defeat the German war machine. Meanwhile, the Republic of Ireland maintained a neutrality that proved very beneficial to the Allied cause.

The Withering of Ireland

During the 1940s and '50s, Ireland fell into a spiral of economic decline and emigration that nearly destroyed the fledgling republic.

IRELAND
in the 1940s and 1950s was the poor child of Europe

When Eamon de Valera presented the new constitution of Ireland in 1937, he hoped it would help create a fully independent and self-sufficient country, free from the influences of Britain or any other nation. However, the tariff walls he erected around the country in order to protect Irish produce actually had the opposite effect. Irish protectionism made the island unappealing to foreign investors, who took their business and their money elsewhere. In response, a lack of jobs started a new wave of Irish emigration that sapped the country of its bright and talented youth.

**JOHN COSTELLO
(1891–1976)**
pushed through the
Republic of Ireland Act

During the war years, most of these problems passed unnoticed by the Irish and their government. War meant lean times for everyone in Europe, and the massive Irish worker migration to Britain appeared to be a temporary, war-related episode. But when the war ended, the truth was revealed. Although most Irish workers returned home after the war, a large number did not. Even more worrying, the Irish continued to cross the sea to Britain to seek employment even after the war.

In 1948, the question of emigration contributed to the downfall of de Valera and Fianna Fáil. For the first time, a coalition government forced out the aging Easter Rising veteran in favour of John Costello as the new Taoiseach. As his first move, Costello pushed through the Republic of Ireland Act, which created the Republic of Ireland as a country outside the British Commonwealth. Despite this largely ceremonial achievement, Costello's government did little to alleviate the economic or emigration problems. In fact, the situation continued to grow worse.

IRISH EMIGRATION

Between 1951 and 1956, the population of Ireland dropped by nearly 200,000 people, to under three million. It was the lowest population for the lower 26 counties of Ireland for over one hundred years. To make matters worse, it was soon discovered that young women were actually leaving the country at a higher rate than young men. (In fact, Ireland's high rate of female emigration throughout its history is nearly unique in the annals of Europe).

With few jobs and poor marriage prospects, women left Ireland in record numbers and most headed for Britain, where jobs such as nursing offered attractive salaries and better chances for meeting potential suitors. This female emigration became so bad that the government began to propose drastic measures such as an age requirement for female emigration or even a large fee. In the end, Costello's government created a 'Commission on Emigration', which spent six years to reach the conclusion that people left Ireland to seek a better life.

Costello's government failed, was replaced once again by de Valera, and then returned to power, but with no one willing to take radical steps to change the situation, the country continued to sink into an ever-deepening spiral of migration and economic depression. In 1954, a book entitled *The Vanishing Irish* concluded that only 30 per cent of the Irish population was married, which was the worst marriage rate in Europe at the time.

Then, in 1957, Fianna Fáil once again returned to power, and de Valera took his seat as Taoiseach. Aged, conservative and nearly blind, de Valera gave in to pressure from within his own party to resign in 1959. Although de Valera was immediately elected president, the attention of the country turned to the new Taoiseach, Seán Lemass. A veteran politician, Lemass possessed the courage and the confidence to enact radical changes that would begin to turn Ireland around.

IRISH EMIGRATION caused a dramatic decrease in the population

The Celtic Tiger

Aided by policies set in place during the 1980s, Ireland's economy skyrocketed in the 1990s and became the prime example for the possibilities of joining the European Union.

**SEÁN LEMASS
(1899–1971)**
became Taoiseach
in 1959

When Séan Lemass became Taoiseach in 1959, Ireland had been suffering from mass emigration and economic stagnation for more than a decade. Determined to turn things around, Lemass found inspiration in the work of Dr T. K. Whitaker. As Secretary of Finance, Whitaker had produced a paper in 1958 entitled Economic Development, which called for the reduction of protective import duties and the enticement of overseas companies to establish manufacturing in Ireland. Lemass immediately set these policies in motion, and the results were nothing short of staggering. For the next five years the Gross National Product

averaged more than 4 per cent growth and emigration dropped to nearly a third of its earlier levels. Once again, Ireland's population began to increase.

The good times didn't last, however. The growth had been aided by a strong British economy, and when this began to crash in the 1960s, it dramatically slowed Irish growth. Still, the Irish continued to look for ways to better their position, and in 1972 over 80 per cent of the Irish population voted to join the European Economic Community (the predecessor of the European Union). Membership brought immediate benefits, such as the Common Agricultural Policy, which granted Ireland subsidies and guaranteed higher prices. Ireland also received funding from European social and regional programmes. Unfortunately, the 1970s saw huge fluctuations in world economic markets and a massive spike in the price of oil, both of which caused economic hardship for Ireland.

When Charles Haughey became Taoiseach in 1980, he warned Ireland that 'we have been living beyond our

THE EEC FLAG was flown when Ireland joined the European Economic Community in 1972

means' and that tough times would be ahead. Haughey's government ruthlessly cut spending, and the results came sooner than anyone could have predicted. Between 1987 and 1993 the Irish Gross Domestic Product rose by an unbelievable 36 per cent, nearly three times the average rate of growth for the rest of the European Union. Suddenly, Ireland had become a 'Celtic Tiger', with its well-educated, English-speaking population attracting corporations from all over the world. By the year 2000, unemployment in Ireland had dropped below 5 per cent and average living standards were estimated to be higher than those in Britain.

Today, Ireland is often used as an example of the benefits of entry into the European Union, and there is no doubt that it is this example that many of the newly joined Eastern European countries are hoping to emulate. However, two important points should not be overlooked: the first is the Irish

DUBLIN
flourished in the late
1980s and early 1990s

THE TIGER'S ROAR

Between 1995 and 2005, Ireland's industrial production tripled, its exports quadrupled and the disposable income of the average Irishman doubled. With its rising prosperity, Ireland made the brave decision to support the new members of the European Union and became one of only three countries in the EU to continue to allow unrestricted access to migrant workers. This move has vastly increased the ethnic diversity in the country.

government taking control of spending in the early 1980s, and the other is the Irish investment in education, which began in the 1950s and 1960s. Without these two moves, membership of the European Union would not have had nearly as great an impact as it has had in Ireland.

Although the effects of the worldwide recession have hit the country as hard as any industrialised nation, Ireland remains in a strong economic position, and still serves as an example of good governance to both Europe and the world.

The Civil Rights Movement and the Troubles

In an attempt to end the religious discrimination and associated violence in Northern Ireland, the Civil Rights Movement became a spark that unwittingly helped to ignite the Troubles.

When Britain created a separate Northern Irish state during the Anglo-Irish War, it made no provision to protect the minority Catholics that made up one third of the population. Unsurprisingly, the Protestants who had long suffered as the minority took advantage of the situation. Using their electoral majority, they easily passed laws which made state schools essentially Protestant, even allowing for discrimination against Catholic teachers. In places where the Protestants were in the minority, such as Londonderry, they rigged the electoral system to get more council housing than Catholics.

At the same time, most Catholics refused to acknowledge the existence of the state.

UVF MURAL
The Ulster Volunteer Force (UVF) was a Protestant terrorist force

Soon, Northern Ireland reverted to a system where the rule of the gun became more important than the rule of the law. The IRA became the defenders of the Catholic population, while the supposedly neutral Royal Ulster Constabulary protected Protestant interests.

IRA MURALS
feature on walls
of some houses
in Catholic areas
of Belfast

Despite the continuing violence that made the country hard to govern, some advancements were made, even for the Catholics. During the 1940s, Catholics received educational help from the government, thus creating an educated Catholic middle class which came into its own during the 1960s.

During this time, much of the funding for the IRA came from America, bringing other ideas with it. This included the Civil Rights Movement, led by Martin Luther King. Seeing a connection between the oppressed blacks in America and the Catholics of Northern Ireland, a group of the new Catholic middle class formed the Northern Ireland Civil Rights Association (NICRA) in 1967. Their goal was to use peaceful protest to overthrow the religious injustice inherent in the Northern Irish Government.

In 1968, the NICRA organised its first march in Dungannon and gathered 2,500 people in protest. Unfortunately, neither the IRA nor the RUC would allow these marches to remain peaceful, and many future marches quickly turned into riots. Although the Civil Rights Movement did eventually win some concessions for Catholics, it also unwittingly helped spark off the Troubles.

MARTIN LUTHER KING (1929–1968) principal leader of the American Civil Rights movement

THE TROUBLES

Everyone seems to know what is meant by the Troubles in Northern Ireland, but an exact definition is hard to find. Essentially, it refers to the ongoing violence caused by the friction between Catholic Nationalists and Irish Unionists in Northern Ireland. Although this violence stretches back for centuries, the start of the Troubles is normally dated to sometime in the 1960s. As the Civil Rights Movement picked up speed, the violence escalated, and both sides adopted terrorism as their main form of political statement. In the major cities, snipers fired on civilians and people dug tunnels through their houses and yards to reach shops and schools. Some Catholic areas became 'no-go' zones for police and military, and were often barricaded by the Catholics. Murder, beatings and gunfire became facts of life.

With the violence spiralling out of control, Britain sent the military to contain the threat and run interference between the Catholics and Protestants. Initially welcomed by the Catholics, the British soldiers quickly proved poorly equipped to deal with the situation, and their heavy handed tactics soon turned the Catholics against them. This violence reached its worst point on 30 January 1972, when British soldiers shot and killed 14 civilians while attempting to make arrests after a banned march. The event borrowed a classic name and became known as 'Bloody Sunday'.

CIVIL RIGHTS
Association march, where British troops made many arrests

After Bloody Sunday, the violence again escalated, and the Government in Westminster, unimpressed by the Northern Irish response, declared Direct Rule over Northern Ireland.

The Good Friday Agreement

Welcomed by most of Northern Ireland's major political parties, the 1998 Belfast Agreement between the United Kingdom and the Republic of Ireland has so far proved to be a major step on the road to peace in Northern Ireland.

Although 'Bloody Sunday' has become an iconic moment in the Northern Ireland conflict, it was just one incident in the bloodiest year of the Troubles, a year that saw nearly 500 people killed in the chaotic violence which engulfed the state. With Westminster having imposed Direct Rule over Northern Ireland, Britain was now desperate to find a way to end the violence. In October of 1972, the British Secretary of State, William Whitelaw, proposed a new constitutional structure that would allow for power sharing among all of the major political parties in Northern Ireland.

Whitelaw's proposal became the basis for a peace conference, held

STORMONT OPENED in 1932 in Belfast. It is where the new Northern Irish Assembly holds its meetings

in Sunningdale in late 1973. All of the major political parties attended (except the violent extremist groups, who were not invited). On 9 December 1973, the representatives signed the Sunningdale Agreement, which adopted Whitehall's system of proportional representation.

GARRET FITZGERALD and Margaret Thatcher signed the Anglo-Irish Agreement in 1985

Although a new power-sharing executive was briefly established, it soon collapsed due to disagreements within several of the parties.

Northern Ireland reverted to a state of barely contained anarchy. From 1977 to 1993 around 100 people died each year in the ongoing Troubles, and thousands more were subjected to pain, fear and intimidation. Eventually, Britain realised that it could not hope to secure peace through unilateral peace talks with the various Northern Ireland factions. Instead, Westminster began consulting with the Republic of Ireland. These talks culminated in the Anglo-Irish Agreement of 1985, signed by Prime Minister Margaret

Thatcher and Taoiseach Garret Fitzgerald. From this point forward, the United Kingdom and the Republic of Ireland would work together to find a lasting solution to the Northern Ireland problem.

While the violence of Northern Ireland continued through the 1980s, the main driving force, the Irish Republican Army, was itself becoming an increasingly political entity through its connections to the modern incarnation of Sinn Féin. This alliance, along with pressure from Britain and Eire, forced the IRA to re-examine the validity of its military campaign. In time, it became clear that Britain could not be bullied into leaving Northern Ireland. Finally, in 1994, the IRA agreed to lay down its arms in order to negotiate a peace.

In 1998, all of the concerned parties met on Good Friday and signed the Belfast Agreement. Although the agreement has faced challenges, it has stood as the most

THE GOOD FRIDAY AGREEMENT

Years of tense multilateral peace talks finally culminated in the Belfast Agreement, signed by the United Kingdom and the Republic of Ireland on Good Friday, 10 April 1998. The agreement contained a number of vitally important statements. First and foremost, there would be no change to the constitutional status of Northern Ireland without a majority vote of its citizens. At the same time, the Republic of Ireland would change its constitution to relinquish its territorial claim over Northern Ireland. Finally, all participants in the agreement would henceforth use only peaceful and democratic methods in the ongoing negotiations.

Less than two months later, the agreement was put to a vote in both Northern Ireland and the Republic. 72 per cent of the Northern Irish voted for the agreement, while in the south an incredible 94 per cent of Irish voted in support.

PEACE TALKS

Tony Blair, Martin McGuinness, David Trimble, John Hume, Bill Clinton, Ian Paisley, Gerry Adams and Bertie Ahern

important step towards peace in Northern Ireland for the last decade. While occasional acts of violence are still perpetrated in the name of Irish nationalism, the frequency has dropped dramatically. Today, Northern Ireland is as safe and prosperous as it has probably ever been.

An Island of Song, Dance and Poetry

Despite its strong economy and increasingly stable government, it is Ireland's cultural exports that have demonstrated the true wealth of the island.

Although the history of Ireland is filled with war, revolution and bloodshed, the present can be viewed as the hopeful dawn of a new golden age. Despite some ongoing troubles in the north, most Irish live in a comfort and safety unknown by any previous generation. Meanwhile, the past champions of Irish culture have helped bring about a resurgence of song, dance, poetry and scholarship unseen since the days of the great monasteries. In fact, probably the most famous Irishman in the world today is a singer who goes by only a single name: Bono.

BONO
was born Paul David Hewson. He is lead singer of the rock band U2

U2

Founded in 1976 by Bono, The Edge (David Howell Evans), Adam Clayton and Larry Mullen, the band exploded on to the rock and roll scene in the late 1970s. Initially, their music was filled with imagery of the violent struggles of Ireland, most noticeable in their 1983 album **War** containing the hit song, '**Bloody Sunday**'. By 1988, the band continued to sing about revolution and political change in their hit '**Pride (In the Name of Love)**'. However, by 2001, the success of the band and the changes in Ireland brought a new sense of joy to their music in songs such as '**Beautiful Day**'. Today, U2 remains one of the world's most popular bands, with 145 million albums sold and 22 Grammy awards. Bono, and the band collectively, have also been praised for their ongoing charity work, especially in aid of Africa.

U2 performing in Cardiff

Northern Ireland has also produced its own musical legend in Van Morrison. Born in Belfast in 1945, Morrison combined traditional Celtic themes with American Rock, Blues and Jazz rhythms to produce a unique sound that has made him one of the world's most popular singer-songwriters. To date, over 150 of his songs have been used in major motion pictures. Morrison has never lost his roots however, and in 1989 he produced the album *Irish Heartbeats,* in conjunction with The Chieftains, a band who are often credited with making traditional Irish music popular again.

Song is not the only ancient Irish art-form to see a revival. In 1994, the Irish dance troupe, Riverdance, received a standing ovation at the Eurovision Song Contest, on their way to becoming the most popular act in the contest's

RIVERDANCE
has helped to promote traditional Irish dance worldwide

IRISH POETRY

Along with song and dance, Ireland has always been known for its poetry; from the ancient bards, through Yeats, to today's champion, Seamus Heaney. Born in Northern Ireland, Heaney's poetry was created in an atmosphere of violent politics, but often focused on the nuances of personal life within this context. In 1995, Heaney won the Nobel Prize in Literature. He is also respected for his work with Anglo-Saxon poetry, most notably his 1999 translation of **Beowulf**.

history. Led by famed dancer, Michael Flatley, the troupe had successful runs in Britain and America and helped bring traditional Irish dance back into popularity.

Of course, all of the people listed above are only the most famous examples. Modern Ireland has become a rich breeding ground for all kinds of cultural pursuits, embracing both traditional and modern art-forms. It is not a return to any mythical golden age; it is, hopefully, the dawn of something new and better.

Index

A

Abbey Theatre   168
Abercromby,
    General Sir Ralph   126
Act of Settlement **95,96,97**
Act of Supremacy   69
Act of Union
        130-134,138,142
Adams, Gerry   241
Ahern, Bertie   241
Alen, John   65
Anglo-Irish Treaty
        202-206,210,214,
        216,218,223
Antrim   215
Armagh   28,33
Asquith, Herbert   **172,173**
Aughrim   102
Auxiliaries   **198,200,201**

B

Balfour, Arthur   **170,171**
Battle of Affane   72
Battle of Bannockburn 55
Battle of Clontarf
        41,42,44.45
Battle of Dundalk   57
Battle of Lime Ridge   152
Battle of the Boyne **98-102**
Beaker people   8
Belfast Agreement
        238,240,241
Belfast Blitz   225
Biggar, Joseph   158
Black and Tans
        197,198, 201,202
Black Oath   85
Black Tom Tyrant   **82-85**
Blair, Tony   241

Bloody Sunday
        198,200-202,237,
        238,243
Bono   **242,243**
Boundary Commission
        205,216
Boycott, Captain   **160**
Boyle, Henry   **112,113**
Brian Bórú **42,43,45,46,63**
Brugha, Cathal   **194,195**
Butt, Isaac   **158**

C

Carrickfergus Castle   **57**
Carson, Sir Edward **123,124**
Castle Chamber   **82,84**
Castlereagh, Lord   **130-133**

Catholic Association 139-141,144
Catholic Emancipation 133,138
Catholic Rent 140
Ceannt, Eamon 187,188
Celtic Tiger 230-233
Celts 10-13,16,18, 22,23-25,32,60
Charles I 82,84,85,86,89,90
Charles II 97,98,103
Chieftains, the 244
Church of Ireland 155
Churchill, Winston 205,222,223
Civil Rights Movement 234-237
Clarke, Thomas 187,188
Clonard 33-35
Clonfert 38
Clonmacnoise 33,38

Coercion Acts 157
coffin ships 148,149
Collins,Michael 197,198, 200, 202,204-213,218
Common Agricultural Policy 231
Confederate Catholics 86-89
Confederate War 89,94
Connacht 55,95
Connolly, James 178-181
Constructive Unionism 170,171
Cork 39
Cornwallis, Lord 129-133
Cosgrave, William 218-220
Costello, John 227,228
court tombs 7,9
Croke Park 200
Cromwell, Oliver 89-95,97
Cúchonnact Maguire 78

Cúchulainn 19
Cumann na nGaedheal 218
Cusack, Michael 162-4
Customs House 209
Cycle of Kings 20,21

D
Dáil 190,192-195, 205-207,211
Dál Cais 40,42
Davis, Thomas 143
de Valera, Eamon 191-195,204-207, 218-223,226-229
Declaration of Independence 114,117
Declaratory Act 116
Defenders 92,120,121
Deirdre of the Sorrows 18
derbfhine 12
Derry 100

Desmond Rebellion **70-74**

Desmond, Earl of **70-74**

Devon Commission **146**

Dillon, John Blake **143**

dissolution of monasteries

18,67,68

Down **215**

Drogheda **8,90-92,101**

druids **14-17,28**

Dublin **32,39,40,43-45,48,**
60,61,64,65,67,88,100,101
105,107,108,118,122,123

Dublin Castle **64,87**

Dublin City Hall **213**

Dublin Lockout **178,180**

Duffy, Charles Gavan **143**

Dungannon **117**

E

Easter Rising **137,153,167,**
176-178,180,182,185

Economic War **222**

Edward Bruce **55-57**

Edward I **54,55**

Edward II **55-57**

Edward III **58,59**

Elizabeth I **70-74,76,77**

Emancipation Bill

138,139,141

Emmet, Robert **134-137**

English Civil War **86,90,91**

English Pale **58,61,65**

Enniskillen **100**

European Economic

Community **231**

European Union **230-233**

F

Famine **56-58,94,110-112**

Fenian Brotherhood **151**

Fenian cycle **20**

Fermanagh **78**

Fianna **20,24**

Fianna Fáil

218,219,227,229

Fili **14,16,17**

filidh **16**

Fisher, J.R. **216**

Fitzgerald, Garret **239,240**

Fitzgerald,

James Fitzmaurice **72**

Fitzgerald, Lord Edward **126**

Flatley, Michael **245**

Flight of the Earls **78,79,82**

Food Vessel folk **8**

G

Gaelic Athletic Association **162-164**

Gaelic football **163,165**

Gaelic League **162,164,165,183**

gallowglass **50-53**

gelfhine **12,13**

General Post Office **181,184,185**

George III **123,124**

George V **203**

Geraldines **47,62**

Gonne, Maud **167,168**

Good Friday Agreement **238-241**

Graces **82,83,86**

Grattan, Henry **122,123, 132,138,139,142,159**

Great Famine **145-150,154,163**

Gregory, Lady Augusta **168**

Griffith, Arthur **191,204-207,218**

Gulliver's Travels **106,109**

H

Handel, George Frideric **111**

Haughey, Charles **231,232**

Heaney, Seamus **245**

Hearts of Oak **120**

Hearts of Steel **120**

Henry II **47,51**

Henry VII **63,64**

Henry VIII **66-70**

Hill of Slane **68**

Home Rule **158,159,161, 170-175,180,183**

Home Rule Association **158**

Hume, John **241**

hurling **60,163,165**

Hyde-Lees, Georgie **168**

I

Industrial Revolution **178**

Iona **35,36**

Irish Citizen Army **180**

Irish Civil War **206-209,216**

Irish Constitution **218,220**

Irish Free State **205,206,212,214,216-218**

Irish Migration **148,149**

Irish Parliamentary Party **172**

Irish Reformation **67**

Irish Republican Army(IRA) **193-203,206209,212, 213,216,235,236,240**

Irish Republican Brotherhood **150,151**

Irish Senate **169**

Irish Socialist Republican
   Party   **179**
Irish Transport and General
   Workers' Union   **179**
Irish Volunteers **156-157**
   175,177,182-183
Irish War of Independence
      198
Irish Workers'
   Textile Union   **179**
irregulars   **208-209**

J

James I   **77-78**
James II   **98-100**
Jerpoint Abbey   **59**

K

kerns   **50-51,53,60**
Kildare   **33,127**
Kildares, the **62-65,67**

Kilmainham Prison **181**
Kilmainham Treaty **160**
Kilwarden, Lord **136-137**
King John   **49**
King, Martin Luther **235**
Kinsale   **76-77,100**
Kitchener, Lord **175-177**

L

Lake, General **126-129**
Land Act
   156-157,160,171-172
Land League   **159-160**
Land Wars
   156-157,159-160
Larkin, James **179-180**
Laudabiliter   **48**
Leinster   **44-47**
Lemass, Sean **229-230**
Limerick   **39-40**

Lionel, Duke of Clarence,
   Earl of Ulster **58-59**
Lloyd George, David
   202-203,205
Londonderry **215,225,234**
longphorts   **39**
Lough Derg   **29**
Lynch, Liam **208-209**

M

Mac Cumhaill, Fionn **20**
Mac Murchada, Diarmait
    46
MacBride, John **167-168**
MacDermott, Sean **188**
MacDonagh, Thomas **111**
MacNeill, Eoin   **164**
Máel Mórda   **44-45**
Máel Sechnaill **43-45**
Maguire, Cúchonnacht **78**

Manchester Martyrs 153,155
Marx, Karl 179
Mathgamain 40,42
McGuinness, Martin 241
Mesolithic era 6,7
monasteries 18,27,30, 32,33,35,36,38,39
Monster Meetings 144,145
Mór, Gearóid 63,64
Mortimer, Roger 56
Munster 42,45,70-73
Munster Plantation 70-73
Murchad 45
Murphy, Fr John 128
Mythological Cycles 20,21

N
Neolithic era 7
New Model Army 90-93
Newgrange 8,9

Niall of the Nine Hostages 23,26
Nine Years War 74,78
Normans 25,33,48,50-53,62
Northern Ireland Civil Rights Association 235
Northern Star 123
The Nation 143,144

O
Oath of Supremacy 82
Obstruction 158
O'Connell, Daniel 138-145,158
O'Donnell, Rory 78.79
Óg, Gearóid 64
O'Mahony, John 151
Ó Néill, Domhnall 56
O'Neill, Hugh 74-79

O'Neill, Owen Roe 88,91,93
Orange Order 118,119,121
Ormond, Earl of 72,89,91,95,98
O'Shea, Katherine 161

P
Paisley, Ian 241
Parnell, Charles Stewart 157-161,170
Partition 214-217
passage tombs 7,9
Patriots 113,114
Pearse, Patrick 181-185
Peel, Robert 147,154
Peep O'Day Boys 120,121
Penal laws 102-106,112,115,124
Phoenix Park 160
Picts 35

pitchcapping 127

portal tombs 7,9

potato blight 146-147

Poynings, Sir Edward 63-64

Proclamation of the Irish
Republic 184

Protestant Ascendancy
105-107,122

Q

Q-Celtic 10,12-13

Quakers 149

Queen Anne 104

Queen Victoria 154,157

R

Redmond, John
172,174-175

Reformation Parliament 67

Repeal Association 144

Repeal rent 144

Republic of Ireland Act 227

Riverdance 244

Robert the Bruce 54-55

Royal Irish Constabulary
196,198-199

Royal Ulster Constabulary
235-236

runes 40

Russell, Lord John 148

the Remonstrance 56

S

Sarsfield, Patrick 102-103

Shawe-Taylor, Captain John
171

Sheehan, Fr john 140

Silken Thomas
(Lord Offaly) 64-65,137

Sinn Féin 190-195,200,203,
206,211,218-220,240

Sitric Silkenbeard 43-44

Society of United Irishmen
122-123

the Squad 197,200,212

St Brendan the Navigator
37

St Columba 35-37

St Columbanus 36-37

St Finnian 34-36

St Leger, Sir Anthony 68

St Patrick 26-30,34

Statutes of Kilkenny 58-59

Stephens, James 150-152

Stormont 238

Strongbow, Richard 47-48

Sunningdale Agreement
239

Surrender and Re-grant
70,74

Swift, Jonathan
106-109,113

T

Talbot, Richard **98-100,103**
Taoiseach **221,227,229, 230-231**
Thatcher, Margaret **239-240**
Thirty Years War **88,92**
Thorough **82-84**
Tigernán **46**
Treaty of Limerick **102-104**
treaty ports **223**
Trimble, David **241**
Trinity College **32**
Troubles **234-239**
Twelve Apostles of Ireland **35-37**
Tyrone's Rebellion **74-75**

U

U2 **242-243**
Ulster Cycle **18-20**
Ulster Defence Force **174-175**
Ulster Plantation **78-81**
Ulster Unionists **173**

V

Van Morrison **244**
Victoria Cross **224-225**
Vikings **25,33,38-45,51**

W

War of the Roses **63**
wedge tombs **7,9**
Wentworth, Thomas **82-86**
Wexford **90,93,128**
Wexford War **126**
Whitaker, Dr T.K. **230**
Whiteboys **118-120**

Whitelaw, William **238**
William III **99-100,104**
Williamite War **98-100,102**
Wogan, Sir John **55**
Wolfe Tone **122-124,137**
woodkerns **81,87,95,119**
Workers' Republic **179**
World War I **173-175,177**
World War II **222-225**
Wyndham, George **171**
Wyse, Thomas **140**

Y

Year of Revolutions **150**
Yeats, W.B. **166-169**
Yeomanry **126-127**
Young Ireland **142-145,150,162**

Further reading

A History of Ireland in 250 Episodes,
Jonathan Bardon, *Gill & MacMillan, 2008*

The Oxford History of Ireland,
R F Foster (Editor), *Oxford Paperbacks, 2001*

Modern Ireland 1600-1972,
R Foster, *Penguin, 1990*

A History of Ireland,
Peter and Fiona Somerset Fry,
Routledge, 1991

The Easter Rising,
Michael Foy & Brian Barton,
The History Press, 2004

The War for Ireland 1913-1923,
Peter Cottrell, *Osprey Publishing, 2009*

Brian Bórú: Ireland's Greatest King?,
Maire Ni Mhaonaigh,
The History Press, 2006

Saint Patrick: His Origins and His Career,
R P C Hanson, *Oxford, 1968*

Modern Ireland, R F Foster,
Penguin History, 1988

For if his balinre once be mou'de, reuenge on them to take,
Which doe our foueraigne Princes lawes, like beaftly beaftes forfake:
Tys not the cruell ftormy rage, nor gathered force of thofe
Nor yet the crooked crabbtree lookes, of greafye glibbed foes,
Can make him to reuoke the thing, his honor hath pretended
But that Dame Juftice muft proceede, 'gaynft thofe that haue offended.

For Mars will fee the finall end, of trayt'rous waged warres,
To plucke the hartes of Rebells downe, that lately pearſt the ſtarres.
To yelde them guerdon for deſertes, by rigour of his blade,
And with the ſame to gall their hartes, which ſuch vproxes haue made
Loe where it is in open fight, moſt perfect to be ſeene
which ſheweth the fatall end aright, of rebells to our Queene.

I Never Knew That About The Irish, Christopher Winn, *Ebury Press, 2009*

Ireland and Empire: Colonial Legacies in Irish History and Culture, Stephen Howe, *Oxford University Press, 2000*

Ireland's Holy Wars: The Struggle for a Nation's Soul: 1500-2000, Marcus Tanner, *Yale University Press, 2001*

The Williamite Wars in Ireland: 1688-1691, John Childs, *Hambledon Continuum, 2007*

Ireland: In the Twentieth Century, Tim Pat Coogan, *Hutchinson, 2003*

Michael Collins, Tim Pat Coogan, *Arrow Books, 1991*

Home Rule: An Irish History 1800-2000, Alvin Jackson, *Weidenfeld & Nicolson, 2003*

Acknowledgments

Published by Gill & Macmillan
Hume Avenue, Park West,
Dublin 12

www.gillmacmillanbooks.ie

ISBN: 978-0-7171-4729-8

This book was conceived, edited
and designed for Gill & Macmillan
by Teapot Press Ltd

Copyright © 2010 Teapot Press Ltd

Text: Joseph McCullough
Editor: Pat Hegarty
Design: Kevin Knight and Sue Rose
Illustrations: Anthony Morris, Lucy Su,
Robin Lawrie and John Rabou

All rights reserved. No part of this publication
may be copied, reproduced or transmitted in
any form or by any means, without the prior
permission of the publishers.

Printed in China

Picture credits

p2. Wexford Pikeman from a 1798 Rebellion
monument in New Ross, Co Wexford.
© Martin Mullen / Dreamstime.
Photos.com: p.14,15,17,23,24,25,27,
31-34,38,40,41,42,49,50,54-59,62,63,66,
68-71, 77,78,90,92-94,96,98-104,106-113,
119,123,124,128,131,132,137,139,140,142,
146,147,150,152,154,155,157-160,166,
171-173,175,179,181,202,203,207,209,210,
214-217,221-223,225,226,229,231-233,238
Wikipedia: p29,36,37,48,52,64,74,83,84,85,
95,102,112,114,116,117,118,125,126,127,129,
130,143,144,162,164,167,168,176,178,
184,185,187,188,191,193,194,196,198,
205,208,211,218
Clipart.com: p.7,10,12,25,26,35,45,51,52,53,
96,97,100,148,190,193,206,213,221,236
istockphoto.com: p.8,47,79
Getty Images: p.165,243,244,245
University of Edinburgh Library: p.73,
254,255
Fotolibra.com: p.75

Every effort has been made to trace
copyright holders not mentioned here.
If there have been any omissions, we will
be happy to rectify this in a reprint.